# THE GUEST IS GOD

## Reflections on Tourism

M.P. Bezbarauh

GYAN PUBLISHING HOUSE
New Delhi - 110002

The Guest is God: Reflections on Tourism

ISBN: 81-212-0884-X

Rs. 540



Published in 2007 in India by
Gyan Publishing House
5, Ansari Road, Daryaganj,
New Delhi-110002
Phones: 23261060, 23282060
Fax: (91) 23285914
e-mail: books@gyanbooks.com

*Laser Typesetting at:* Best Computers, Delhi
*Printed at:* Salasar Imaging System, Delhi

*To*

*ILA and SHIV*
*The Future*

# Contents

# Preface

This book is a collection of some of my many lectures and presentation in national and international fora during my long tenure in the Ministry of Tourism and thereafter. As a background, it is necessary to recount some of my experiences during these years.

Bureaucrats are forever trained to be faceless-the system is important, not the individual. If inspite of such training for long years I am breaking the basic tenet, to speak about my years in the Ministry of Tourism, it is only because I have often been specifically requested to recount my years in the Tourism Ministry. In any case five years of association is a long one and some personal impact of such association is inevitable. Therefore, I seek indulgence for talking in first person.

It was, for me, a journey of learning and exploration. I soon realised two important things. First, that tourism is a very well known subject, always talked about in any gatherings, but there is little awareness about the fine nuances of tourism. Such lack of awareness is widespread. Second, tourism is a multidimensional activity which-needs involvement of many players. To understand Tourism I tried to study the subject in depth. The result was my first book "Indian Tourism beyond the millennium" which was so well received by the industry and the academicia alike.

With this background, we in the Ministry set about therefore with the first and foremost job of creating awareness. This resulted in the awareness campaign aimed at the common people who are such vital links in tourism. The theme of this campaign, launched with the help of PATA was, 'tourism touches everyone.'

Drafting of a new tourism policy was a two-pronged strategy. No doubt we needed a new policy which was in tune with the new economic philosophy . But more than that we wanted a national debate on tourism. We departed from the usual practice of keeping the draft a secret document and instead shared it widely with all concerned. And with what results! It is a different matter that because of political changes, and other factors beyond my control the policy still was going through the process, till 2002. But it was intensely and widely debated and discussed. In the process it achieved its primary objective of creating awareness. Tourism became the 'in' thing.

With the same objective we decided to observe a National Tourism Day. A day was found—the date on which the department was born—and we built around this day a celebration for a week, the highlights of which were the Foundation Day lecture and the Tourism Expo. Since 1998, we had international luminaries like Mr. Antonio Savignac, former Secretary General Emiritus of the World Tourism Organisation, Mr. Frangialli, the present Secretary General of the WTO, Mr. Martin Brackenbury, Chairman of the Business Council of the WTO. The National Tourism Expo was to integrate the efforts of different agencies trying to showcase India and create one platform of international standard. We aimed to make it the biggest tourism expo east of the Suez.

Awareness needed information to be disseminated. We found that information on what the government was doing was scanty. For the public, getting information was a difficult process. Initially, we intended to bring out an in house bulletin. It took time to take shape. Then we had financial problems. One way out of the problem was to try collaboration with the private sector without any cost to the government. That is how 'Explore India' was born. It has grown a lot since inception *and* has changed its colour a bit too. After the successful Incredible India campaign it charged its name too. However I am sure that it will remain a source of information and exchange of ideas between the centre, state governments and the private sector, and will retain the primary objective of disseminating information and educating the people.

Internationally this was a period of great satisfaction for me. Apart from the distinction bestowed on me by The Pacific Asia Travel Association (PATA) by unanimously making me their Chairman, getting the PATA annual conference to India was a matter of great satisfaction. In the WTO, India continued to be in the prominent position, having been elected to the Executive Council for the fourth term consecutively.

Naturally, in the Indian context government plays a key role in tourism and coordination among the various ministries of the government is important. But it is also difficult. Again and again we found that good intentions foundered because of lack of appreciation by those who had a role in it. For creating a national agenda for tourism a common platform was needed. This realisation led to the constitution, for the first time, of the Group of Ministers and the Committee of Secretaries, with some very good results. The decision on Export House status to tourism sector, and on principle acceptance of visa on arrival, for example would not have been possible but for this system of coordination.

One long pending demand of the private sector was creation of a public private partnership platform. One major step in this direction was the creation of the Board of Tourism Trade and Industry. Soon it was felt that a restructuring of this body was needed to make it more effective. Happily, the Prime Minister himself had given direction about the creation of a new Board/Committee. The private sector was however always involved in all that was essential, to the extent that a major action plan for tourism was drawn up entirely by the experts from the private sector. One notable achievement of PPP was the creation of a society called the "Experience India." Its members, prominent leaders in tourism industry contributed voluntarily a portion of their foreign exchange earnings, to create fund for a "brand" marketing of India. It was the first attempt for a large scale marketing of India.

Five years is too short a period in the life of a nation. However one feels happy for having contributed to the elevation of tourism to the rightful place in the national agenda. During this period the sector got the blessings of the P.M. who graced four of the tourism functions, emphatically reminding the nation of the important role of tourism in his Independence Day message. And that 'feel good' atmosphere continued in the budget speeches of the FM and after a long time tourism got pride of place. One could not wish for a better farewell gift.

As I said in my lecture in India-EU Business Summit, tourism now seems to be "business" in India. I am delighted because all my efforts in the last ten years of active association with tourism has been devoted to creating that space for tourism in India and not to consider it as an "invisible" that just happens.

Naturally, my wife has shared the joys as well as some pains at times of this last journey of my career. Her common sense criticism have often added strength to my observations.

I am grateful to Amit Garg of Gyan Publishing, but for whose persistence the book would not have seen the light of day.

# *PART I*

# GLOBAL TOURISM

# 1

# The Long Quiest for Sustainable Development*

"Whatever I dig of you, O Earth,
May you of that have quick replenishment!
O Purifying one, may my thrust never
Reach right unto your vital points, your heart!"

—*Hymn from Ancient Indian Scripture, the Vedas*

"How can you buy or sell the sky, the warmth of the land? The idea is strange to us. Yet we do not own the freshness of the air or the sparkle of the water...Every part of this earth is sacred to my people. Every shining pine needle, every sandy shore, every mist in the dark woods, every clearing and humming insect is holy in the memory and experience of my people...."

—Chief Shealth of the Suwanish tribe of American Indians in reply to President Pierce's request to sell his land-what is now the State of Washington—to the government.

## The Quest

These two expressions of concern for the environment and ecology, almost 4,000 thousand years apart, indicate that the quest for sustainable development as a concept has been very old and continuing. Yet, visible and collective international action on sustainable development has been confined to the last part of the 20th Century. The flurry of activities and

* Presented in the meeting of the Strategic Group of World Tourism Organization. Alexandria 23 June 2001.

discussions on the subject crammed into the short period between the Bruntland Commission's report on 'Our Common Future' in 1987 and the World Summit in 2002, is a testimony to the realisation of the urgency of the matter.

This paper briefly analyses the salient developments in the field not for sustainable development per se, but primarily focussing on the concept in relation to tourism.

Some of the landmarks on the subject are—

1. 1972— UN Conference on the Human Environment, Stockholm.
2. 1980— Manila Declaration on World Tourism.
3. 1987— The Report, 'Our Common Future' defining the concept of sustainable development.
4. 1992— The Rio declaration and the adoption of Agenda 21 an agenda for action.
5. 1996— Adoption of Agenda 21 for Travel and Tourism industry.
6. 1997— Male Declaration on Sustainable Tourism development; Manila Declaration on the Social Impact of Tourism; Resolution of the 19th Special session of the UN General Assembly Requesting the Commission on Sustainable Development to develop an Action—oriented international programme of work on sustainable tourism in co-ordination with the WTO, UNEP and other UN agencies.
7. 1998— Resolution of the UN General Assembly proclaiming 2002 as the International Year of Ecotourism as well as the International Year of the Mountains.
8. 1999— WTO General Assembly accepts the Global Code of Ethics; The UN Commission on Sustainable Development takes note of the Global Code of Ethics and expresses interest in it.

9. 2001— UN General Assembly adopts resolution emphasizing the importance of responsible and sustainable tourism and takes note of the Global Code of Ethics with interest.
10. 2002— World Summit on Ecotourism.
11. 2002— World Summit on Sustainable Development.

There are numerous other sectoral events and initiatives on various components of sustainable development, like coastal areas, biodiversity, environment, culture, prevention of child labour and child sex and the like. On the cultural side, which is closely linked to tourism, the International convention for the Protection of World Cultural and Natural Heritage in Nairobi (November, 1972), and the charter drawn up by the International Council on Monuments and Sites (ICOMOS) in Brussels 1976, can be mentioned.

The developments so far highlight two major trends. First, the WTO has been consistently pursuing the importance of sustainable tourism and its relevance within the wider concept of sustainable development. In fact the Manila Declaration of 1980 can be termed as the pathfinder on the subject, much before the world had taken serious note of the importance of the concept of sustainability. Second, unfortunately the pioneering initiatives of the WTO remained largely confined to the tourism sector only and till recently the world community at large had not taken note of the impact of the tourism sector on the issue of sustainability.

**Tourism: Overlooked?**

Till 1997 the issue of sustainable tourism was not independently and seriously discussed in the UN system. The Commission on Sustainable Development discussed this subject only in relation to the small island developing states. Even the much lauded Rio declaration was heavily environment focussed and did not mention tourism as such. Agenda 21 did take tourism into account but not in an integrated manner. The UN General Assembly in its 19th Special Session, while reviewing the progress of implementation of Agenda 21, however, acknowledged the importance of tourism and placed tourism in the agenda of the Commission. The commission in its seventh session in 1999 organised a multi-stakeholders' dialogue on sustainable tourism and accorded the status of an economic sector to tourism. One significant decision of this Commission was to draw up an international work programme on sustainable tourism, a decision WTO should be closely associated within implementation.

This late recognition of tourism in the context of sustainable development efforts is surprising but understandable to some extent. Surprising because tourism and environment have a symbiotic relationship. It is well recognised that travel and tourism promote awareness about environmental issues. A well-managed tourism can add substantially to environmental sustainability. And tourism itself requires a high quality environment and eco–system for its sustenance. Many tourism destinations flourish only because of the quality of their environment. In a sense the earlier preoccupation with environment and ecology served the ends of tourism as well.

Yet it is not difficult to understand this neglect of comprehensive tourism issues in the quest for sustainable development if one looks for rational explanations. Though tourism arrivals increased ten fold between 1970 and 2000, in the early 80s the negative effects of tourism had not yet shown too strongly. The primary concern those days were for the environment and ecology, and tourism was not seen as a great spoiler. Moreover, tourism is a complex, multi-dimensional multi-sectoral activity. While the generic term tourism might have escaped the attention of those who were planning for sustainable development, it is possible that many of the components of tourism were adequately addressed in these initiatives.

**The Concept: Need for Clarity**

Sustainable development covers so many diverse aspects within its fold that any attempt to define it must risk the danger of either stating too much or too little. However the principles enunciated in the Brundtland Commission's report remains till today the most comprehensive exposition of the concept. It defines sustainable development as "development that meets the needs of the present without compromising the ability of future generations to meet their own needs." Further it says, "In essence, sustainable development is a process of change in which the exploitation of resources, the direction of investments, the orientation of technological development, and institutional change are all in harmony and enhance both current and future potential to meet human needs and aspirations." This basic principle has been further elaborated in the Earth Summit in Rio in 1992. Agenda 21 gave shape to these objectives by drawing up an exhaustive action programme.

This definition also naturally has its share of criticism, not always unfounded. One criticism of a more philosophical nature is that, for wider acceptability, the concept should be more positive. The objective of sustainable development should be, it is argued, to enable each generation to enrich the inheritance. Use of resources should not be seen in too restrictive a sense. The development process involves use of resources. Stability of resources should be maintained in some aggregate macro sense and need not necessarily be too restrictive in every use in every place.

Sustainable development, it is said, should go beyond the concern for the physical to societal and cultural values. The thrust of 'our common future' it was felt, did not adequately reflect the pressing concerns of poverty and economic sustainability. Fortunately, the Rio Declaration and the exhaustive Agenda 21 rectified these weaknesses by putting poverty concerns at the core of the action programme.

On the other hand, the WTO attempted a definition of the concept of sustainable tourism way back in 1988. As it followed the report of the Brundtland Commission, it did have the influence of the wider definition on sustainable development. "Sustainable tourism development", it says, "meets the needs of present tourists and host regions while protecting and enhancing opportunity for the future. It is envisaged as leading to management of all resources in such a way that economic, social, and aesthetic needs can be fulfilled while maintaining cultural integrity, essential ecological processes, biological diversity, and life support systems."

This definition attempts to be specific and comprehensive but apparently fails to meet the expectations of the UN system agencies. Decision 7/3 of the 7th Session of the Commission on Sustainable Development calls upon all the major groups, the UN system agencies, Governments, WTO and others to "clarify further the concepts of sustainable tourism and eco-tourism."

The most pressing problem of sustainable development in the world today has been tardy implementation. The ideas need wider acceptability and understanding, particularly at the grass-roots level where philosophical debates and ideology pale in relation to hard realities. The first basic requirement is to frame the concept and action agenda in terms understandable to the targeted society and related to their environment and ethos.

**The Gap between the Idea and Action**

As the world prepares to review the progress of action ten years after Rio, there is candid admission that despite domestic and international actions there is still a major gap in the implementation of Agenda 21. Papers of the preparatory committee for the World summit recognize this gap. The Summit will have to chart out the strategy for the future on the basis of the shared experience of the past.

The background papers for the Summit recognize the need to "promote sustainable tourism development in order to increase benefits from tourism resources for the population in the host communities, and maintain the cultural and environmental integrity of the host communities." In the 198 action points drawn up there are many in which tourism can directly or indirectly contribute but the role of tourism has been specified only in relation to the Small Island Developing States. Naturally, as in the past the primary concern is with the physical environment.

Many questions need to be asked if one wants to frame a strategy for the future.The need for sustainable development is universally accepted. Yet why do unsustainable practices come about? Why do those who are to implement sustainable practices sometimes meet failures? Are they unwilling or incapable? It is necessary to look at underlying causes rather than the symptoms. Policies are most effective when they look at the root causes.

For a long time beneath the general acceptance of the concept there was simmering difference, if not conflict, in vision among the developed and the developing and underdeveloped nations. Many activists saw the growing concern for sustainable development as the rich countries' self interest and attempt to take away attention from the pressing problems of hunger, poverty, malnutrition and so on. For example, the Second Citizen's Report on the State of India's Environment in 1985-86 had clearly voiced this apprehension. "One lesson is" it says, "therefore clear: the main cause of environmental destruction in the world is the demand for natural resources generated by the consumption of the rich...". In the 1972 UN conference such views were strongly aired. The Brazilian delegation had said "smoke is a sign of progress". And India's Prime Minister Mrs. Gandhi's statement—"poverty is the biggest polluter" was quoted again and again. Since 1972 things have changed. Growing realisation of the needs of sustainability, greater efforts of the word organisations to bridge the gap in perception and changing economic realities in recent times have modified the content of action agenda and have narrowed the misapprehensions.

The World Development Report of 1992, for example, categorically states that there is strong evidence of links between poverty alleviation and sustainable goals. The World Summit in Rio recognised this imperative and Principle 5 of the declaration regards "eradication of poverty as an indispensable requirement for sustainable development". Agenda 21 logically identifies many action points for poverty alleviation as part of sustainable development strategy. However by now it is recognised that independent action on poverty falls short of the desired effect. As early as 1984 the UNEP in a report had pointed out the adverse effects of heavy debt burden and adverse terms of trade on the environment of the Third World. There is growing realisation that the strategy for sustainable development must be based on an integrated socio-economic planning. The 7th meeting of the Commission on Sustainable Development in 1999 emphasized the need to link sustainable development to an integrated strategy for poverty reduction. It urged governments to "maximise the potential of tourism for eradication of poverty by developing appropriate strategies in co-operation with all major groups, indigenous and local communities." As noted earlier, the World Summit later this year does not seem to be working on the same perception of a role for tourism in the integrated economic development strategy for poverty eradication. This is an area which the tourism community and the WTO could push with vigour. Analysis of tourism data shows that in most countries with high levels of poverty, tourism has a significant contribution to the GDP and has potential of substantial further growth. This development may have two implications—the happy one that tourism is becoming the change agent for economic development; or the unhappy possibility that in this quest of using tourism as a tool for development , sustainable concerns can be relegated to the background. There is greater need therefore, of integrating the sustainable tourism initiatives to the overall sustainable development strategies.

This drawback of the sustainable development strategies so far, has been mentioned by the Second Citizen's Report on the State of India's Environment—"there is a major problem with the entire range of activities and concerns: it does not appear to be based on a holistic understanding of the relationship between environment and the development process in this country. The prgrammes are ad hoc, without clear priorities ...". Tourism concerns, for example, however well intentioned they are, if pursued in isolation, may not find much fervour at the aggregate level. There are too many sectors trying to do too much at the same time. Agenda 21 is a comprehensive action document but it runs to almost 300 pages of action points. As a result, there is lack of focus and confusing overlapping of agencies, each pursuing it's own agenda. Almost all discussions in recent times have underlined the importance of integrated and co-ordinated action at the field level. The 1999 decision of the Council for Sustainable Development had advocated an integrated work programme. For successful implementation of the strategies, this should form the first and most important agenda of action.

Both the Travel and Tourism Agenda 21 and the Global Code of Ethics are refreshingly focussed, clear and brief. Even then they gain more acceptability and become easier to implement if the WTO succeeds in integrating them to the general agenda of action.

Similarly, quite often sectoral and rigid approach of the stakeholder groups cannot only create difficulties in implementation of the agenda but also can defeat the very objectives. One can mention the experience in Andaman and Nicobar Islands in India. A comprehensive tourism development plan for the island was drawn up with the assistance of the WTO and UNDP. However the project had to satisfy very detailed scrutiny of the environment agencies which took time . In the meantime environmental degradation for expanding tourism, which was not properly planned and regulated, went on. The dilemma was that while there was no check on unsustainable activities by private persons, the tourism department's intention of planning sustainable development stumbled at the rigid interpretations of sustainable norms.

Implementation also has not been satisfactory because in

most cases yardsticks for assessing implementation are deficient or lacking. In most cases there is no accountability for non-implementation. The WTO has done pioneering work by developing a set of guidelines for local planners and for monitoring various sustainable tourism norms. The next step is to motivate the national governments to accept these guidelines and use them extensively and to build in some form of accountability at every stage for non-performance.

**Action: The Perception So Far**

For any discussion on sustainable development the Earth Summit and the Rio declaration and Agenda 21 that followed from it are taken as landmarks. The Rio Declaration has 27 principles and the thrust of the principles are—

1. Human beings are at the centre of concern for sustainable development.
2. The right to development must be fulfilled so as to equitably meet environmental and development needs of present and future generations.
3. Environmental protection should be seen as integral part of development and not in isolation.
4. Eradication of poverty is an integral part of the requirement.
5. Global partnership is needed.
6. Public awareness and participation are important elements of the strategy.
7. Effective environmental legislations should be put in place.
8. Indigenous people and local communities should have a vital role in the implementation of sustainable development strategies.

Agenda 21 followed as a detailed comprehensive plan of action grouped into 40 chapters and more than 100 separate action areas. This wide ranging programme of action was adopted by the 182 countries that participated in the Conference.

The WTO followed it up by an agenda of its own called Agenda 21 for Travel and Tourism Industry. It identified nine priority areas for governments, NTAs and representative trade organisations and ten priority areas of action for the industry. The clearly focussed priorities give it an edge over others in implementation. The Travel and Tourism Agenda 21 (TT Agenda 21) identifies three core tools which can be used for achieving the objectives—

(a) regulations;

(b) free market mechanism;

(c) industry-led voluntary programmes.

The TT Agenda itself points out that regulations should play only a supportive role. Over regulation often confuses the issues, and often become ineffective unless there is a strong and efficient mechanism for monitoring their implementation. One of the grievances expressed in the Second Citizens Report on the State of the Environment in India was that there was "too much of a policeman's attitude" in managing sustainable development. More than 200 central and state laws existed at that time. This was not proportionate to the benefits derived from them.

The TT Agenda itself calls the other two proposed tools unusual. It refers to some good examples of the market delivering the desired objectives. The Secretary General of WTO in his address to the second Tourism Summit in Geneva in 2000 had indicated how the market can work. The market chooses the desirable. "A survey by a major German bank revealed that one out of every two travellers attached importance to environmental quality in choosing a holiday destination."

Unfortunately the developing and underdeveloped countries suffer from many market imperfections. Leaving sustainable management to the market may, it is feared, in some cases aggravate the malady. As is often said in the developing countries, use of such measures must be tempered with a human face. In fact the background paper on the Local authority perspective prepared for the Seventh session of the Commission on sustainable Development in 1999 states the fear more strongly—"...the primary barrier to sustainable development through tourism is an over reliance on market mechanisms to guide tourism development and consumption decisions. The market...is insensitive to many requirements of sustainable tourism." In particular, reliance on the market may be disadvantageous to the poor countries and can work as an indirect trade barrier.

The UN General Assembly, in its resolution on tourism in the 19th Special Session, had advised the Commission on Sustainable Development to look at tourism as one of the largest industries and fastest growing economic sectors. The key areas of action identified in the resolution are—

1. Develop an action oriented international programme of work on sustainable tourism;
2. Develop shared interest of all the stakeholders;
3. Pay special attention to the relationship between environmental protection and conservation and sustainable tourism;
4. Strengthen national policy development and enhance capacity in the areas of physical planning, monitoring, use of regulatory mechanisms, information, education and marketing;
5. Assistance of the international community including the international financial institutions in achieving the above objectives.

These directives effectively cover the most important areas of action for sustainable tourism in the coming years. The primary question today is, how to ensure their compliance in a realistic time bound action plan?

## The Future: What Needs to be Done?

The Secretary General of the WTO in his address to the World Tourism Summit in Geneva in 2000 had stressed—"today sustainable development is seen as a necessary concern; tomorrow it will be an inescapable requirement." The problem with tomorrow is that it never comes and we can always be moving into that inevitable calamity in a relaxed anticipation devoid of urgency. The tomorrow is almost on us and we have to face the realities.

## Global Problem, Global Action

To quote the Secretary General again—"the concept of sustainable development is global by definition. The 'future' is inevitably 'common'. It has been pointed out that world peace, sustainable development, world market for goods and services are examples of international public goods. They will be under provided without conscious, collective and concerted action.

All the reports and resolutions of the UN and other related organisations that we have examined have strongly urged for international initiatives on sustainable tourism involving all the UN agencies. This co-ordination mechanism has to be formalised and put in place.

Clause 10 of the decision 7/3 of the Commission on Sustainable Development invited the UN and the WTO to *jointly facilitate the establishment of an ad hoc informal open-ended working group on tourism* to address all the issues mentioned above. The working group should function immediately and effectively.

## Shared Interest and Shared Responsibilities

*Sustainable development as such, and sustainable tourism in particular, is multi-dimensional. Institutional mechanisms must be put in place to develop and articulate the sense of shared interest at international, national and local levels. WTO should take the pro-active role to advocate an institutional mechanism at the international level of all the stakeholders, including tourism.*

*Resolutions of the UN and of the Commission on Sustainable Development have repeatedly advocated coordination among various UN agencies for sustainable tourism development.*

To prevent wastage of efforts and resources, as well as to avoid duplication, integration of the action plans to the extent possible should be attempted. Sustainable tourism projects succeeds more if they are not in isolation. A case study of sustainable city—tourism in Heidelberg has established that—

(a) Only the integration of the activities for a sustainable tourism into an overall city concept e.g. the local Agenda 21 or a city development plan, can produce visible success;

(b) Isolated measures to the sole benefit of tourism are not accepted by the population. The most important features are the networked projects.

The EC has developed this integration into a specific policy. EC policy for the development of tourism must mesh with Article 6 of the Amsterdam treaty according to which the protection of the environment must be integrated to the Union's other policies in order to promote sustainable development."

**International Funding for Sustainable Tourism**

There is unanimity among all agencies on the importance of international financing institutions playing a specific and important role in furthering sustainable development initiatives. The UN General Assembly Resolution 44/228 of 1989 is categorical on the subject. It directs the UN Conference on Environment and development to (a) identify ways and means of new and additional financial resources, (b) quantify financial requirements, (c) identify means of supporting developing countries in their efforts for sustainable developments. Agenda 21 has clearly spelt out the dimensions of the steps to be taken.

Now that the UN has clearly' accepted tourism as an important economic sector contributing to poverty eradication and environmental preservation, the WTO should make concrete its sustainable development plans for additional international financing in two stages. The first is for its own international integrated initiatives involving all their tourist sector interest groups. The second is to help performing nations to expand their sustainable tourism activities. By financially encouraging good work of some countries the WTO will be able to inspire the others.

In all cases of direct financing of projects by international financial institutions, can the agreement also include a clause that a few key parameters of sustainable tourism would be implemented by the receiving country?

**Help Capacity Building**

The UN General Assembly resolution on Sustainable Tourism emphasizes the importance of strengthening national policy development and capacity building. It is widely recognised that many national governments are unable to implement sustainable tourism not because of lack of interest, but because they do not have the technical and managerial know-how. International communities and organisations like the WTO's support for capacity building of national organisations have to be structured, well defined, comprehensive, co-ordinated and continuous. It can be conceived in two levels. First, a comprehensive approach to assist the developing countries to establish national frameworks of policies and priorities. WTO should give preference in its programme implementation to—

(a) Capacity building;

(b) Human resource development;

(c) Technology transfer;

(d) Exchange of knowledge and information.

Additional funding for such schemes should be sought for from the international funding agencies under integrated projects for poverty eradication and environmental and socio-cultural preservation through tourism.

### Build Regional Cooperation

The other level could be based on the experience of the EC. It shows that regional cooperation can be effective for exchange of good practices and experiences. Regional projects can be most useful where economies of scale can be achieved, like in the fields of training, statistics etc. They are effective where joint solutions to shared problems are possible or where shared interest in the field of product development lead to mutually profitable results. Studies in the EC have shown that regional approach should focus more on the common aspects rather than trying to bring in too many areas.

### Start a Campaign for Local Travel and Tourism Agenda 21

Agenda 21 has to be translated from a distant international concept to the people's own charters. Involvement and participation of the local and indigenous people is essential for the success of sustainable development concept. The Heidelberg city example also shows the importance of local Agenda 21. It has been reported that in more than 2000 communities in 64 countries Agenda 21 partnership institutions already exist. As a conscious policy, tourism should be built into these. A programme to expand local Travel and Tourism Agenda as part of the sustainable development dialogue should form part of the WTO's work plan.

### Encourage Comprehensive Sustainable Strategy and Not Partial Approach

Due to either ignorance or to lack of clarity of the concept of sustainability tourism, in many places there is an attempt to concentrate on part of it. Efforts to develop alternative forms of tourism, like eco-tourism, while laudable, may divert attention from the basic necessity of a commitment to the integrated sustainable development steps.

### The Demand and Supply of the Tourism Product

The problems of sustainable tourism can be seen from two angles—supply and demand. On the demand side most of the unsustainable behaviour of the tourists arise from either ignorance of the local customs and norms or from what is called the 'away from home syndrome'. In either case the need is for creating awareness and education.

On the supply side the major problem in most developing countries is what is termed as the 'irridex' effect—the irritation caused to the local population because of diversion of services in short supply for the use of the tourists. There is also the potent problem of overuse of the physical and non-renewable resources for economic gains from tourism. In many cases action is wanting either for ignorance or lack of capability.

Action to counter these trends has to be sharp focussed. In the developing countries, it will be primarily to build capacity and enhance competence. The developed countries produce the largest outbound tourists. Education, awareness and preventive steps should start in these countries as well.

**Implementation is the Key**

"Between the idea
And the reality
Between the motion
And the act
Falls the Shadow"

*T.S. Eliot*

The long quest for sustainable development has aroused global interest in the future of man's journey in this planet. It has brought together the international community to deliberate on a common strategy of development for our common future. Much has been achieved but much more remains to be done. The issues have been exhaustively discussed and debated. Action agenda has been drawn and redrawn. But implementation has been slow and inadequate. It is now time to get down solely to the issues of implementation. As philosopher Albert Camus said in a different context—"I shall tell you a great secret, my friend. Don't wait for the last judgement; it takes place everyday."

# 2

# Global Strategy for Tourism 2020*

> "The trouble with our times is that the future is not what it used to be."
>
> —*Paul Valery*

> "We are entering an Age of Unreason ... a time when the only prediction that will hold true is that no prediction will hold true."
>
> —*Charles Handy*

So fast and unpredictable have been the changes in the later part of the 20th Century that planning long term strategy has become highly vulnerable. There are delightful stories of many famous predictions going totally wrong.

— In 1943, Chairman of the IBM, Thomas Watson is reported to have said that there would be market for about five computers.

— Even in 1977, Ken Olson, Chairman and founder of the Digital Equipment Corporation was quoted as saying that there was no reason why anyone would like to have a computer at home.

— The famous Decca Music Company reportedly rejected the Beatles in 1962 thinking that "guitar music was on the way out."

## Managing Change

It is commonly said that while agricultural revolution

* Presentation in Monaco World Summit on "Globalization and Development". Monte Carlo. 27-29 October 2004.

took centuries and the industrial revolution was telescoped into less than half of that, the technological revolution of 20th Century is changing every decade. "Technology is developing at an ever accelerating rate of speed with each new technology compounding the speed and capability of those that came before." (John Naisbitt—'Global Paradox')

During the 90s, it is said, 46 per cent of the Fortune 500 companies just disappeared. Making future strategy therefore requires very careful study of the trends. In that sense strategy to manage uncertainty and to adapt to change should be the foundation of future action. Darwin had pointed out long back that those who adapt, survive. Global strategy today should primarily centre around steps to create capacity to mange change and uncertainty.

**Implementation is the Key:** 'between the idea and the reality... falls the shadow'.

This century has also seen tremendous proliferation of information bringing home the truth of Eliot's cry—'Where is the wisdom we have lost in knowledge,

Where is the knowledge we have lost in information?'

More information has been created since the 70s in this world than was available since the dawn of civilization. Managing this mass of information for the common good of mankind should be the first step in any global strategy. There have been extensive discussions on the future of tourism and the strategies to be adopted for making tourism sustainable and serve the wider concerns of mankind. One does not always feel reassured that implementation of the accepted ideas and strategies has been uniformly good. More than a decade back at Rio the world had charted out the course of future action for survival. Tourism was not directly part of it, but the spirit of Rio was the soul of tourism for the future. In 2002 at Johannesburg again close to hundred thousand stakeholders, policy makers, intellectuals gathered to discuss the common future of mankind. The World Tourism

Organization formulated the Code of Ethics which has now been adopted by the United Nations General Assembly in 2001. It is now necessary to devise a mechanism for the world community to be able to monitor and evaluate how these good intentions have been implemented across the globe. The first global strategy therefore suggests itself—how to implement what the world has accepted as the basic need for our common future?

**Global Strategies: Some General Issues**

Strategy, by the very connotation of the word, is a tool to achieve some definite objectives. Global strategy should therefore address the larger concerns of mankind and should be designed to meet the emerging challenges.

*Globalization—an inescapable reality:* Many forces that shape the development of the world in the new millennium, like technological innovations, spread of knowledge, financial integration and trade liberalization have truly made the world a global village. These forces accentuate, as the World Development Report, 2000 says "the growing global interdependence across space, time and issues." Globalization, it is accepted universally, is an unavoidable corollary of human development saga, but not necessarily always an unmixed blessing. This consensus is reflected in the UN Millennium Declaration which says, "we believe that the central challenge that we face today is to ensure that globalization becomes a positive force for all the world's people. For while globalization offers great opportunities, at present its benefits are very unevenly shared, while its costs are unevenly distributed."

It is admitted that globalization has done much good to the world. Closer integration of countries and peoples of the world has reduced the sense of isolation. It has given the developing countries quicker access to information and technology than was possible earlier. Trade liberalization has made it possible for goods, services, knowledge, technology and capital to move more freely than before. Resultant reduction in cost of transportation and communication has enabled many countries to grow faster.

But, points out Joseph Stiglitz, winner of Nobel Prize in Economics ('Globalization and its Discontents'), "if, in too many instances, the benefits of globalization have been less than its advocates claim, the price paid has been greater, as the environment has been destroyed...as rapid change has not allowed countries time for cultural adaptation."

The Human Development Report, 1999 also brings attention to this flip side of globalization—"the collapse of space, time and borders may be creating a global village...but billions of others find borders as high as ever."

Stiglitz agrees, and so does everyone that the process is irreversible. There is broad agreement that to reap the benefits of globalization and to avoid its pitfalls, global collective action for global goods are needed. In the arena of tourism, WTO as the global institution, has the responsibility of making globalization work for the poor. Tourism as a dynamic force for globalization, must be made a vehicle for global action for sustainable development. Such policy should also encompass action to create capacity for the nations who are now lower on the development scale so that they are capable of participating in the global action for exploiting the benefits of globalization. The 'Code of Ethics' must be pursued as an instrument of global action and Tourism Local Agenda 21 should be at the forefront of WTO's action programme for the future. Stiglitz says—"if we are to address the legitimate concerns of those who have expressed a discontent with globalization, if we are to make globalization work for billions of people for whom it has not, if we are to make globalization with a human face succeed, then our voices must be raised." WTO has the responsibility of raising the voice of the tourism nations.

The world is now engaged in intense discussions on the modalities of trade liberalization. The developing countries and the LDCs are hoping that the process of liberalization with a 'human face' in the service sector will bring them more optimism for growth. At the same time, more non-tariff barriers are growing in tourism. Adverse travel advisories, restrictive visa policies and offensive security drills are causing continuous frustration to many countries. If the global institutions like the WTO succeed in evolving a dignified, rational and non-discriminatory system of removing these non-tariff barriers to the process of globalization, without making any compromise on the requirement of security, global strategy in tourism would have achieved the greatest breakthrough.

*The basic thrust of any global strategy should therefore be to devise policies and institutions to meet this fundamental challenge posed by the forces of globalization.* Such global strategy should be capable of reflecting all the diversity of common humanity while striving to create a shared future.

*Other side of the coin-localization—think global, act local?* There is wide variety around the world in the way people are, the way they think and the way they work. Recognition of such variety strengthens the fabric of global action, and that fabric is woven by the thread of what is increasingly being called the spirit of "localization". The concept of localization underscores the basic philosophy that macro policies must take into consideration the local nuances and variations. Localization reflects the increasing desire of people to have autonomy in their own governance in consonance with local conditions, culture and aspirations. As Naisbitt again puts it beautifully, "the bonding commonality of human beings is our distinctiveness".

*Think in totality and not in isolation:* Technological developments and globalization has not only made the world interdependent, but different human objectives are so much related to each other that full achievement in any one sector is not possible without their horizontal integration with other related sectors. Global strategy in tourism, for example, will be less than optimal in effectiveness unless issues of environment, civil aviation, cultural preservation and security are woven around it.

*Increasing competition, need to facilitate capacity to compete:* The Report of the Secretary General of UN to the General Assembly on the implementation of the Millennium Declaration has shown that even among the developing countries there is wide divergence in capacity to take action on the strategy to combat the fundamental problem of poverty. Any global strategy at macro level must take into account this basic reality. Global strategy for any sectoral development must make assessment of this variance in capacity and provide for measures to create capacity where required.

In fact because the problems to be tackled are so big, and the capacity to implement varies so widely and because it is desirable that the possible solutions should take care of the local variations, the concept of global strategy itself is often viewed with skepticism. But experience also has shown that taking a global view often increases the possibility of success of policies even at local levels. As the Human Development Report, 2003 points out, UN agencies like the WTO have a role to play, more specifically in areas like—

- *"To monitor progress globally;*
- *Track progress nationally;*
- *Identify key obstacles to goals and solutions;*
- *Engage broad segments of society around the world through the millennium campaign."*

### Poverty—The Overwhelming Question

Poverty undoubtedly is the primary challenge of the millennium. The assembly of nations—the General Assembly of the UN— has tried to give expression to this concern by resolving to eliminate poverty and to halve, by the year 2015, the proportion of world's people whose income is less than a dollar a day. Eradication of poverty is, fittingly the number one goal of the Millennium Development Goals. It is also quite apparent that concern for poverty is also at the centre of all other millennium goals.

Different terms have been used at different times to express mankind's concern about poverty and to take steps to attack the problem. Throughout the later part of the last century, when the problem of development and consequently the problem of poverty attracted global attention, the expressions of mankind's resolve almost sounded apologetic or diffident. The words like "reduction" and "alleviation" mostly used to refer to national and international policies on poverty appeared like an open admission that the problem was to big to be tackled. Nowadays the UN uses both "elimination" and "eradication" as the objective of poverty programmes—both implying 'complete removal' in dictionary sense. This change in approach gives more vitality and dynamism to the approach and more of optimism. *However, it is important to keep in mind that the global strategy for eradication of poverty must develop systems and institutions that ensure that once eradicated the spectre of poverty does not rise from the ashes again.*

*"Shameful" dimensions of poverty:* The extent of poverty has been well documented and the stark reality of failure of action of the global community prompts WTO to term the statistics as 'shameful'. ('Tourism and Poverty Alleviation'—WTO). Here are some of the distressing statistics recorded by WTO—

- Globally 1.2 billion people live in 'extreme consumption poverty';
- Over sixty per cent of the world's poor live in just five countries—China, Nigeria, India, Ethiopia and Bangladesh;
- More than 800 million or 15% of the world's population suffer from malnutrition;
- Every minute one woman dies of pregnancy and childbirth.

- Eight out of every 100 infants don't live to see their fifth birthday.

*The most disconcerting part of the problem is that such large scale poverty has coexisted with remarkable growth in the world economy and the rich-poor gap is increasing.*

- During the last decade of the 20th Century when total world income increased by an average of 2.5 per cent annually, the number of people living in poverty actually increased by almost 100 million.
- The World Development Report, 1999 gives the historical perception and the enormity of the problem with the following facts—
    - (a) 60 countries of the world were getting steadily poorer since 1980 till the end of the century;
    - (b) The gap between the richest and poorest was about 3 to 1 in 1820, 11 to 1 in 1913, 35 to 1 in 1950, 44 to 1 in 1973 and 72 to 1 in 1992.
- The World Development Report, 2000 brings out the grim and worrisome picture with telling facts. "The average per capita income of the poorest and the middle thirds of all countries has lost ground steadily over the last several decades compared with the average income of the richer third...In fact, rich countries have been growing faster than poor countries since the Industrial Revolution of the mid-19th Century. A recent estimate suggests that the ratio of per capita income between the richest and the poorest countries increased six fold between 1870 and 1985. Such findings are of great concern because they show how difficult it is for poor countries to close the gap with their wealthier counterparts."

Tourism—the largest industry, can play a positive role:

The importance of tourism for employment generation and income creation has been extensively documented and universally accepted. At the national level, tourism, both domestic and international, can reach far flung areas and provide employment without much investment. Globally, tourism flows from the rich to the poorer countries can have the effect of redistribution of income in favour of the poorer countries. The developing countries can utilize tourism more as a tool for fighting poverty. While this effective role of tourism is recognized and should be more encouraged, one has to be careful not to project tourism in isolation as the only or even the primary weapon. Tourism is only one of the means of attacking the problem of poverty. Considering the wide complexity of the problem of poverty, WTO has rightly advocated an integrated multi-dimensional strategy where tourism is an important input. In order that tourism can play an effective role in national policy for poverty elimination, it must be integrated with the activities of other sectors in the overall national planning model.

*Tourism impact "invisible":* Unfortunately, even in countries which have the problem of poverty to tackle urgently, tourism does not seem to be getting the importance it deserves in their development planning. For example, India has a very high incidence of poverty which has not shown much improvement in spite of conscious planned efforts by the government. In India tourism earns the second highest amount of foreign exchange for the country and tourism potential of India gives it a comparative advantage. Yet, a survey at the beginning the new millennium by World Travel and Tourism Council of 160 countries in terms of government expenditure on tourism, places India at the lowly position of 156.

In most cases tourism seem to grow on its own with little or no help from the government and that may explain the seeming apathy of national tourism administrations. At the same time there is not enough awareness in most countries about the importance of tourism because the tourism impact is often not visible. In the national accounting system of India, for example, such receipts are grouped under the heading 'invisibles'. No amount of general advocacy for tourism can have the same impact on policy makers as cold statistics of tourism's direct and indirect impact can have. *WTO is advocating use of Tourism Satellite Accounting System (TSA) to overcome this deficiency and to bring out the real impact of tourism. TSA should be not just advocacy but part of a definite, holistic global strategy to fight the menace of poverty.*

Similarly at the local level the benefits of tourism often do not percolate to the needy to the extent they could because the mechanism for their *participation is often not in place* or are inadequate. Various reasons may explain this inability of local level people to participate. They may be left out of participation because—

- They do not see the benefits of participation;
- There are no institutional arrangements for their participation;
- They do not have the capacity to participate.

While the process of participation will have to be locally planned and designed, taking into account the local variations and characteristics, *global strategy on this important area should be to—*

(a) Global intervention to create awareness on the importance of local participation;

(b) Devise mechanism for formal platforms for participation, for example, spread the concept of Local Agenda 21 as a necessary global commitment;

(c) *Create mechanism for global intervention to empower the poor countries—like assistance for capacity building through Human Resource Development, institutional networking to provide financial and technical assistance to those who need.*

*Hopeful signs—'tourism becoming globalized.'* WTO brings the happy report that compared to 1950, tourism is now spreading far and wide. In 1950 top 15 destinations in the world accounted for 87 per cent of the arrivals which came down to 75 per cent in 1970 and 60 per cent in 2001.

Added to such spread of tourism is the optimistic trend that in the poor and developing countries which need tourism to tackle poverty, tourism is now growing faster than in the developed countries. Let us look at some of the heart warming figures quoted by WTO ('Tourism and Poverty Alleviation—Recommendations for Action")—

- The growth rate in international arrivals to low and lower middle income countries between 1990 and 2001 was 97.5 per cent;
- Amongst the 30 countries with largest poor populations, there were ten countries with a growth in international arrivals between 1990 and 2001 of over 200 per cent.
- In 2002 tourism was the primary source of foreign exchange earnings in 49 least developed countries (LDCs).
- Tourism is one of the principal exports of 83% of the developing countries and the principal export of one-third of the developing countries.
- Tourism receipts as percentage of GDP is very high in may countries, e.g., 57.7 per cent in Maldives, 27.4 per cent in Vanuata and 17 per cent in Samoa.

*But many concerns and long way to go:* While these developments are encouraging there are some disconcerting notes, which highlight the fact that determined efforts are still needed to make tourism truly a vehicle of development for large numbers who are still deprived.

(a) First, it has to be realized that the statistical performance does not truly reflect the micro picture. As the developing countries started their progress from a very low base, the percentage growth naturally appears very promising. But in macro and absolute numbers they add up to very little.

(b) WTO figures show that even in 2001 the top 15 countries received 60 per cent of the total arrivals.

The WTO projection for 2020 also does not show any remarkable change. Top ten destinations, mostly developed countries, are likely to account for about 50 per cent of both arrivals and receipts. Apparently in spite of good progress in the LDCs the globalization of tourism touches only the fringe of the problem of poverty and the gap between the poor and the rich continues. Tourism has potential of working towards equitable distribution of wealth by causing redistribution of income from the rich to poorer nations. But apparently the process has been slower than what is possible to achieve and therefore definite action are required to enable the poor and developing countries to take benefit of the potential of tourism as a tool for poverty reduction.

(c) The statistics also point to another area of concern—in these countries there is mismatch between arrival and receipts. As the WTO report puts it—"although low income countries are getting a high share of growth in arrivals, this is not matched by a similar share of growth in receipts." Between 1990 and 2001 the Low Income Countries achieved 110 per cent growth in arrivals but had only 52 per cent growth in receipts.

(d) Many of the developing and poor countries are also experiencing high growth of outbound tourism. This may be a natural corollary of development and growth in income for the people. But it also implies that the net effect of tourism growth may not be as impressive. In fact, the higher reverse flow of tourism may create overall adverse terms of trade in tourism sector. This is reflected in India where the outbound growth has been faster than the inbound.

It is obvious that the expectation that tourism growth may globally help in reducing the rich-poor gap at macro level and help in redistribution of wealth among nations has not been realized to the desirable extent. The global strategy and the strategy of the global institutions like WTO should be to positively intervene to empower the developing nations and the LDCs. The work programmes should be designed with definite objectives of, first, strengthening the positive trends and. second, helping the countries to overcome the negative ones. Of the many options available for the global community and global institutions to work towards that end could be—

(a) To increase the efficiency of the tourism services, enabling to earn higher returns and greater value addition to the products;

(b) To help overcome the infrastructural and other inadequacies of the developing countries and LDCs so that they can achieve higher rates of growth continuously to reduce the gap with the developed countries.

WTO's present work programmes are broadly based on such objectives. But they are grouped regionwise, which does not reflect the relative need of the countries or the extent of their backwardness. *To achieve closer monitoring and focus on the countries which are poor and need more attention than others, it would be a good idea to group the countries based on their needs rather than on geographical positions for the limited purpose of poverty elimination strategy. For all other purposes the present geographical arrangements may continue.*

Considering that the role of tourism in poverty elimination is universally accepted, the *funding needs of the LDCs and developing countries for tourism development infrastructure should be broad based.* The cost of technology is high and without quick infrastructure and technological developments these countries will remain at a disadvantage. There are valid reasons for higher infusion of resources to achieve quicker growth. There is no reason why World Bank funding for tourism infrastructure should be a low priority.

If world peace has to be viable this problem of poverty has to be tackled and the process of widening rich-poor gap has to be reversed. This was the conclusion of the Pearson Commission 30 years ago and this is the recommendation of Nobel Prize winner in economics, Prof. Tinbergen, in recent times. WTO should therefore devise more proactive policies to encourage tourism growth in the poor countries.

***Sustainable Development of Tourism***

> "a necessary concern today-inescapable requirement tomorrow".

That is how the Secretary General of the WTO cautioned the world in the World Tourism Summit in Geneva in 2000. The problem with 'tomorrow' is that it never comes and we can always be moving into that inevitable calamity in a relaxed anticipation devoid of urgency. Four years from that and in this Summit again, tomorrow is almost on us and the realities have to be assessed with urgency.

In the euphoria of tourism growth during the last decades it is possible that the concern for sustainable tourism gets diluted and the adverse impact of uncared , unplanned tourism is overlooked. In a candid admission of common failure of the global community of this front, President Jacques Chirac of France had sounded the warning bell in Johannesburg— "Ten years after Rio, we have no reason to celebrate. The implementation of Agenda 21 is a long, hard road. Awareness of our failure to act should lead us, here in Johannesburg to conclude the global alliance for sustainable developmentit... Our house is burning down and we are blind to itit...If the whole humanity was to behave like the Northern countries, it would take two more planets to satisfy our needs."

*"Poverty is the biggest polluter"*. This of quoted statement of Mrs. Indira Gandhi in the UN Conference on Human Environment in 1972 brings out the two crucial implications. First, poverty and sustainable development are deeply interlinked. Second the perception of the poor countries, grouped then as the 'third world', was strongly critical of the

hypocrisy of the rich world. The strongly aired view in the UN Conference was that the main cause of the environmental destructions of the world was the demand for natural resources resulting from the consumption of the rich. The message for the global community that has flowed from many subsequent conferences is equally clear—that the serious concerns for sustainable development must be sensitively harmonized with the overwhelming challenge of the problem of poverty. The onus of making it happen, of giving shape to the concrete plans drawn up by various world meets and of providing resources required to do so, largely rests with those nations which had the advantage of early start in the development history.

Way back in 1992, the World Development Report pointed out the strong links between poverty alleviation and sustainable goals. The World Summit in Rio recognized this imperative and Principle 5 of the Declaration regards "eradication of poverty as an indispensable requirement for sustainable development".

*Needed—a holistic approach.* Both poverty and sustainable development issues are multi-dimensional, the parameters cutting across many sectors. While too many people and organizations around the world are trying to do a lot in their own respective ways, in national and global plans, a holistic approach is often missing. The 7th meeting of the UN Commission on Sustainable Development in 1999 emphasized the need for integrated action. It urged tha governments to "maximize the potential of tourism for eradication of poverty by developing appropriate strategies in cooperation with all major groups, indigenous and local communities." This decision had also advocated that *an integrated global work programme be drawn up for sustainable tourism.* In the tourism sector the 'Global Code of Ethics' has been a step in that direction. But it is only a code, dependent on many factors and players for its success, and not really a plan of action that the world needs. The WTO had also done pioneering work in developing a set of guidelines for local planners and for monitoring various sustainable tourism norms. The next step should be to motivate the countries to implement them and monitor such performance on a continuous global basis. WTO could devise some norms in consultations with the National Tourism Administrations, for linking the work programmes and other assistance, to performance in the sustainable norms.

The Travel and Tourism Agenda 21 of WTO is another effort to carry forward the message of sustainable tourism, but it again has remained largely recommendatory. It identifies nine priority areas for the Governments and NTAs and ten such priority areas for the private sector and industry. The core tools identified for achieving the sustainable objectives are—

1. Regulations;
2. Free market mechanism;
3. Industry led voluntary action.

The limitations of these tools however should be kept in mind. Regulations sometimes can be self-defeating if they take the dimension of "too much of a policeman's attitude" as the Second Citizens Report on the State of the Environment in India complained. The Agenda itself admits the limitations of the market approach to guide sustainable concerns. This concern was also voiced by the 7th Session of the Commission on Sustainable Development in 1999 "...the primary barrier to sustainable development through tourism is an over reliance on the market mechanisms to guide tourism development and consumption decisions. The market is...insensitive to many requirements of sustainable tourism."

The UN General Assembly in its resolution on Tourism in the 19th Special Session had identified few key areas for action which could now be taken up and translated into action plans for global action as part of a global strategy—

1. Develop an action oriented international programme of work on sustainable tourism;

2. Develop shared interest of all stakeholders;
3. Pay special attention to the relationship between environmental protection and conservation and sustainable tourism;
4. Strengthen national policy development and *enhance capacity* in the areas of physical planning, monitoring, use of regulatory mechanisms, information, education and marketing;
5. Assistance of the international community including *international financial institutions* in achieving the above objectives.

The last suggestion about international funding was mentioned by the UN long back and assumes importance today. The UN General Assembly resolution of 1981 was in fact specific on the subject. It directed the UN Conference on Environment and Development to—

(a) Identify ways and means of new and additional financial resources;
(b) Quantify financial requirements;
(c) Identify means of supporting developing countries in their efforts for sustainable development.

The Agenda 21 has detailed recommendations on implementing these suggestions for international funding. These recommendations are equally applicable to tourism as well in view of the links between tourism, poverty elimination and sustainable tourism.

***Human Resource Development***

> "We must open the doors of opportunity. But we must also equip them to go through those doors."
>
> *Lyndon B. Johnson*

Globalization and spread of tourism has made the world a global village. Ideas move more freely than before as does expectations of travellers about the content and quality of services. Changes in consumer behaviour, socio-demographic developments and technological developments have combined to make the 'consumer the king' and to bring in a new era of "experience economy". The nations trying to exploit the new found strengths of tourism are constantly in great competition with each other.

All these factors underline the great importance of Human Resource Development (HRD) in any future global strategy for tourism. Technological developments are fast engulfing all aspects of human existence. Technology is also changing fast, much faster now than it ever did over the centuries. But technology itself does not empower. The capability to comprehend the power of technology and the ability to use it for one's advantage is what provides the winning edge. These developments are going to influence the dimensions of future HRD in many ways—

1. In order to keep pace with the changes in technology, the skill imparted should be such that can change quickly with time. It is also recognized that the guiding concept of the future human resource development should be to develop multi-disciplinary skills.
2. The training needs of the countries will have to be so designed that they can quickly adjust to changing technologies.
3. The globalization process has opened opportunities for more labour mobility. But the benefits of such opportunity can be availed only by those who have the access to latest technologies. The developing countries trying to take advantage of this are at a disadvantage because they do not have access to latest technologies or cannot keep up with the fast changes. According to the WTO, one-third of the world's population does not have access to new technologies either as producer or as users, because acquisition of latest technology is costly and fast obsolescence puts heavy pressure on the finances of the poor countries.

4. At the same time the fast changes in technology implies that the human resources have to be on a 'continuous training mode'. Skill up gradation of this nature is also a costly proposition, often beyond the capacity of many nations who have other areas of priority for spending scarce resources.

*HRD—some constraints.* Even if tourism has made the world a global village and trade liberalization has opened up possibilities of movement of tourism professionals, tourism education and training still lacks harmonization. The concept of an inter-connected world depends immensely on harmonization of tourism education and its quality.

At the national level, most of the developing countries have given inadequate attention to tourism human resource development primarily because of financial constraints and party because tourism is seen as a private sector responsibility. Some of the fall out effects of such neglect are—

1. There is mismatch between demand and supply of trained persons. Investments in HRD in most places have not kept pace with the requirements. As a result trained persons are not available to provide the quality of service the modern travellers are demanding. Moreover in most cases the trained manpower are confined to the organized sector only, leaving out a vast unorganized sector, composed mostly of small operators who provide very important services in the rural and non-metro areas.
2. Because of this mismatch and increasing demand which the government efforts are not meeting, thère has been mushroom growth of private sector training institutions. They are not properly supervised and regulated and being individual, ad hoc initiatives, they lack proper technology, equipments and qualified teachers to provide international standard education. Often, their course contents cater to localized demand. The standards and quality of education are not

properly monitored. In such situations uniformity in testing and certification systems cannot be achieved.

HRD has been long recognized as one of the important areas for global initiatives and positive intervention by global institutions. The Human Development Report, 2001 had made a forceful plea for such action—"building technological capacity in developing countries is central to forging long term solutions because technologies for development have not, cannot and will not be supplied through the global market place alone."

*International and regional networking:* The number of institutions of excellence imparting tourism education is very limited, touching only a miniscule of the total requirements. Most of these institutions are confined to the developed countries. Among the many possible options for global action in this area, two strategies can be highlighted. First, as recommended by the Conference of Tourism Professionals jointly organized by WTO and ESCAP *"develop regional models of education and training appropriate to various countries, culture...."* As an example of Public Private Partnership that is often talked about, *five regional institutes of HRD could be set up in the five continents with collaboration of industry—hotels, travel trade, civil aviation etc.—and joint efforts of WTO, UNDP, WTTC, UNESCO, WB, ICAO, EU etc.* The regional institute could—

- Network with identified national institutions;
- Provide them research strength;
- Provide training and other facilities to upgrade the learning of the faculty;
- Help in harmonizing the course materials for the region.

The national organizations in their turn, could, with guidance and monitoring of WTO, internally develop PPP schemes to network national institutions in similar lines. This will achieve regional and international harmonization, standardize quality of training and reach largest number of people whose capacity to employment will be enhanced.

*Training of Trainers:* Even with such efforts, the problem is so huge that only its fringes will be touched. Large number of service providers who are crucial to the total image of the 'experience' of the country will still be left out. The problem of poverty is so acute that when tourism provides opportunities to overcome them, it will be a pity if they are not enabled to take advantage of the opportunities. In the short run, and the short run is important as mankind is losing crucial time to tackle the ticking time bomb—the best way out to handle the problem is a programme of 'training of trainers'. WTO should spearhead a training of trainers programme at the regional level with effective involvement of the industry who would be the main beneficiary of the programme. This will be a worthwhile initiative of the WTO-BC and when fully operational, the programme can be taken over by the national governments or the national industry organizations.

***Fear of Flying—The Crowded Skies***

*Need for synergy:* The development of tourism since late sixties of the last century shows the crucial role civil aviation plays. The tragic events of 9/11 and the plunge that tourism took immediately thereafter also points to the significance of close synergy between tourism and civil aviation. Even today tourism has not fully recovered from the wide ranging impact of these events on aviation industry and business. The fear of flying and the subsequent security concerns affect the long haul destinations more than others.

Among the many steps taken to prop up the aviation industry, industrialized states have subsidized their development routes in their domestic markets. WTO believes that such analogy should be extended to the international sectors as well to facilitate poor country destinations. In a globalized, liberalizing market place, poor country routes are de facto socio-politically equivalent to their domestic route and similar treatment should be given. Integrated global action for tourism development should cover such collaboration with the aviation sector to achieve globally desirable goals.

The tourism boom reaching 1.6 billion tourists by 2020 and all the other technological developments in civil aviation technology making travel faster and bigger also brings dimensions of air safety to be closely looked into globally. The projected growth of international air traffic passengers, doubling from 1.4 billion in the coming years, will naturally make the air corridors very crowded. More crowded will be the domestic routes. Going by the WTO statistics of ratio of 1:7 between international and domestic travellers, by 2020 there will be 10 billion domestic travellers, large proportion of whom will travel by air. Air traffic safety and management therefore assumes greater importance than before. It is feared that many developing countries will not be able to match the investments required to acquire or upgrade continuously the air safety equipments, and will lose in competitiveness. *There should be a global strategy for harmonized action to help the disadvantaged countries to implement air safety norms and regulations, technology improvements and training of personnel.*

***Tourism—creating a movement for peace.***

*"Travel is the language of peace"* —*Mahatma Gandhi*

In 1915, the Russian artist Malevich gave expression to the eternal quest of the human mind for peace and 'presented the unpresentable sublime' by painting a white square on a white background. "I have beaten the lining of the coloured sky, torn it away and in the sack which formed itself, I have put colours and knotted it. Swim! The free white sea, infinity, lies before you."*

By the end of the century, tourism created the biggest movement of people around the globe seen in human history. And the people hoped that this language of peace would prevail over the clutter of weapons. Such hopes were shattered rudely in the new millennium when tourists have been used on many occasions as the shield for terrorism. The last straw was in the tragic 9/11 when the very symbol of modern tourism—the aircraft—was blatantly used as the weapon for mass destructions.

The constitution of UNESCO in 1945 significantly stated that "since wars begin in the minds of men, it is in the minds of men that the defences of peace must be constructed." We need now a strategy to shape the minds of the tourists as a weapon against war and destruction. The young are the best to shape and therefore WTO's awareness campaign globally must address the youths in schools and colleges with the explicit message of tourism as a language of peace.

Culture is one of the strongest motivations for travel. Culture in all its diversity is the strongest binding force for peace. Celebration of year 2000 as the International Year for Culture of Peace is a very worthwhile beginning and should be developed from a one year effort to a movement of mankind to thrive for peace continuously. Individually the tourist may not be so aware of the capacity of his contribution to the collective movement. The faith of each tourist in peace, his desire to understand the realities and the human feelings of the places that he visits, can be given shape and language for a movement. Can each ticket the tourist holds, for example, also contain a pledge to uphold the ideals of peace and to contribute to it?

An old Chinese proverb says—even a thousand mile journey has to start with the first step. The global community can take the first steps, small though they may be. The process of globalization has made the need for action more pressing than ever before.

---

* Chakraverty, Sauvik : Antidote. Essays against Indian Socialism.

# 3

# Future HR Needs for Tourism*

Changes in modern times are taking place so fast and in such unpredictable ways that talking about the future has always the attendant risk of being proved totally wrong. There are delightful stories about how some famous people went totally wrong. Thomas Watson Chairman of the IBM is reported to have said in 1943 that there could be world market for about five computers. Even in 1977 Ken Olson Chairman and founder of the Digital Equipment Corporation was quoted as saying that there was no reason why anyone would want a computer at home. It was reported that during the decade of the 90s, 46% of the Fortune 500 companies disappeared. Change is and has always been a part of evolution but changes have been more rapid than before. While making an assessment of the future HR needs, one has therefore to be very careful to understand the future trends.

The future HR needs in the travel and tourism sector will no doubt depend on the way the sector evolves in the future. In spite of the fast changing scenario, it is possible to visualise the emerging and compelling influences that are likely to shape the growth of the sector in the coming years. If we understand the nuances of these influences and trends, we can make reasonable assessments about the HR needs of the industry in the future.

*Presented in PATA Annual Conference, New Delhi, 14 April 2002.

## Expanding the Supply Base

"We must open the doors of opportunity. But we must also equip our people to walk through those doors." Lyndon B. Johnson.

The quantum of growth of the travel and tourism industry is one of the most important determinants of the future requirements. International tourists arrivals have grown ten times during 1970 and 2000. During the last two decades it has consistently grown at a rate higher than the rate of growth of the world economy. Tourism has become the biggest industry in the world but the growth potentials are immense, because at present only about 7% of the capable travellers are actually travelling. The recent events of September 11 have cast a temporary shadow over the industry, but after a careful assessment of the situation so far, the World Tourism Organisation (WTO) has maintained its earlier projection of growth to reach a figure of 1.6 billion arrivals by 2020.

During this period direct jobs in tourism has been about 4 percent of the total. Tourism jobs have been growing 1.5 per cent faster than the world average for the past 15 years. There is no doubt that tremendous opportunities will be created for employment in the tourism sector as it advances in the projected growth. The first challenge before the planners is to match the great expansion in demand by creating capacity for supply. As there is always a lag in putting in place the institutional framework to develop human resources, matching supply with demand and ensuring the equitable spread of such facilities around the globe so that all regions can equally benefit from the tourism boom, will be the first challenge of the future.

## Globalisation

It is commonly said that tourism has made the world a global village. Ideas move more freely than before and so does expectation of the travellers about the content and quality of services. There is therefore greater need for harmonisation of the content of HR education patterns and for international standards and norms to be dovetailed to the domestic demands and culture.

But the more important impact of globalisation is that it will change the pattern of travel and tourism industry and the manner of doing business. International economic liberalisation process has dismantled the barriers to free trade and the technological developments have made it possible for tourism business to go beyond the borders. For example, E-ticketing has changed the organisation of travel industry, virtual reality experience has modified the concept of marketing, internet information availability has altered the way information is disseminated and has empowered the consumer, computer reservation system has facilitated the service to be provided.

The WTO had projected sometimes back that these developments would result in a few major structural changes in the travel and tourism business.—

1. horizontal integration of business, forcing out small and medium operators through economies of scale;
2. vertical integration through acquisitions, strategic alliances;
3. emergence of global multinationals in tourism business partly as a result of the above developments;
4. emergence of an industry comprising broadly of two categories of players, a small number of global operators and a small number of "niche" operators catering to the specialist segments.

Such structural changes in the way that business is managed will certainly change the structure of HRD initiatives. Few implications are obvious. First, the course contents and the approach will have to be altered, to be in tune with the requirements of a globalised industry. Second, as the primary purpose of the HR education is to serve the emerging needs of the industry, linkages with the industry will have to be even stronger if education is to be purposeful and employment oriented. Third, the industry will have to directly get involved in the growth of this sector more than before.

**Technological Developments**

The most profound impact on the future developments of the tourism sector and therefore on the future HR needs, it is universally accepted, will be of fast changing technology and its all encompassing sweep of all spheres of human activities. The technological developments are characterised by two distinct developments. First, they are swiftly covering all aspects of human life more than ever before. In particular, the spread of information technology has changed the nature of man's command over information. It is stated that more information has been produced since the 70s than was produced since the beginning of human civilization. To dramatize the total impact, John Naisbitt in his book "the Global Paradox" has quoted Randall L. Tobias former vice chairman of AT&T to narrate the following story— "A theologian asked the most powerful supercomputer, Is there a God?' The computer said it lacked the processing power to know. It asked to be connected to all the other supercomputers in the world. Still, it was not enough power. So the computer was hooked up to all the mainframes in the world, and then all the minicomputers, and to all the personal computers. And eventually it was connected to all the computers in cars, microwaves, VCRs, digital watches and so on. The theologian asked for the final time, Is there a God?' And the computer replied : There is now!" The second characteristic of technological developments, which also creates problems for HR planning is that technology is changing nowadays at a rate much faster than it did over the centuries. As Naisbitt puts it "Technology is developing at an ever-accelerating rate of speed, with each new technology compounding the speed and capabilities of those that came before."

Such developments condition the type of future educational needs for the tourism sector. Firstly, the training needs will have to be so designed that they can adjust to changing technologies. Training will also have to be a continuous process and the industry will have to upgrade skill of its employees more often than now as well as provide for refresher training. Secondly, in the international scenario, with greater labour mobility made possible by the globalisation process, the manpower can be trained in modern technologies only if the countries have access to such technologies. It is essential, in order to increase the competitive edge of the human resources to empower them with the capability to acquire the best of tools that fashion the industry. The developing countries trying to enter the information age is confronted with this problem as one-third of the world's population, according to the WTO, do not have access to the new technologies either as producers or as users. The future HR needs are inextricably linked up to this problem. Thirdly, the primary focus of tourism education in the future will have to be to teach people how to adapt to change. Those who adapt survive, said Darwin long ago. That message is very pertinent in the tourism education today, and will be increasingly important in the future. "If you do not change, you can become extinct" is the main theme of Dr Spencer Johnson's best selling book 'Who Moved My Cheese' and that is the key to tourism HR needs of the future.

But technology itself does not empower. The capability to comprehend the power of technology and the ability to use it for one's advantage is what provides the winning edge and that is what human resource development will have to aim at in the future. Skill development is the basic objective of any human resource development strategy. In order to keep pace with the new technology, the skill imparted should be such that can change quickly with time. It is recognised widely that the guiding concept of the future human resource development should be to develop multi-disciplinary skills or in brief, multi-skills. It is not only the compulsions of technology, but employers are also going for multi-skilling as a cost saving device. Prof. Chuck Gee in his address in 1999 to the ESCAP/WTO seminar on HR challenges for the future, pointed out that this change was going to be a permanent feature of the future scenario. In fact in the future it will have to be pursued more as a policy of human resource development to attract and retain bright people to the industry. Prof. Gee has pointed to a phenomenon that was seen during every crisis that the industry faced—the Asian financial crisis, and the recent fallout of the September 11 events—that, the first reaction is to cut jobs. Employers tend to look for multi-skilled employees to reduce cost and minimise worker turnover, and employees find such skills give them better job security.

The assessment of the hospitality industry also largely corroborate these trends in human resource development for the future. Prof. Gee has referred to the findings of the International Hotel and Restaurant Association which has identified, on the basis of research in over 20 countries, some of the important variables for preparing managers for the future as- -

1) manage change;
2) blend functional skills;
3) possess a high degree of technology savvy.

**The Consumer is the King—Age of Experience Economy'**

If the technological developments empower the individual to demand goods and services with more information and facility at his command, some socio-demographic developments have further strengthened the power of the consumer in the present situation. The new age traveller is a typical example of time poor, money rich' syndrome. He makes more trips in a year than before but of shorter durations, and is more discerning about the quality of service that he demands and the experience he expects. The new trend in travel and tourism where the tourist demands more of an experience has been described by the Harvard professors, Joseph Pine and James Gilmore as the 'experience economy'. It is not sufficient only to provide the best quality of services the totality of such services should also be able to create a memorable experience for the person. Such experience being essentially personal and individualised, the transition to the experience economy, it is said, brings in the concept of 'a market of one.' This is the market that the future human resource development strategy should be able to tackle, by training the service providers to service an experience.

Added to this need of training people to the highly specialised job of servicing the individualised market is the need to cater to the complexity of highly segmented markets. The motivations for travel are becoming more and more diverse and increasing competition among the competing destinations has enlarged the choice of the consumer. The future training needs therefore must cover all these diverse requirements.

### A Holistic Approach to Tourism Management

It appears contradictory that while the training of human resources has to tackle the highly specialised demands of the individualised customers, such training also has to be viewed as a total management concept that can cover the complexities of the diverse segments of the market. But the experience to be created for one individual is the totality of a large number of services and products, mostly inter-dependant. A multidisciplinary approach is essential because many of the tourism resources are used by others as well. Tourism defies any simple explanation. It is a very sensitive sector and small changes in the social, economic and cultural situations may affect the total tourism services. On the other hand, because of its impact, unless sensitively developed, tourism promotion may adversely affect the culture, ecology and environment of a place. The adoption of a Global Code of Ethics is a reflection of the growing concern for developing sustainable tourism in this world. This concern is likely to be the single-most important issue of future tourism development. No piecemeal approach can satisfactorily resolve the problems of sustainable tourism. Tourism development has to be viewed as a total management concept encompassing the problems of design, of product development and of the management of the services and the behaviour of the tourists as well as the host community. A tall order though it is, the human resources development for tourism in the future must take into account the development of a total manager.

**The Constraints**

The constraints in tackling the future HR needs are too many and they differ from place to place. A recent conference of the senior functionaries of the Asia Pacific region organised by the ESCAP and the WTO highlighted the following as the major problems. These constraints, with minor variations perhaps will hold true for most other countries—

1) Mismatch between demand and supply—the investment in HRD in most places has not kept pace with the requirements. As a result the trained personnel are not available to provide the quality of service the new developments are demanding. Moreover in most cases the available manpower attend to the organised sector only, leaving out a vast unorganised sector, composed of very small operators, outside the concern of both the government and the private sector. In the future, the effects of this mismatch is likely to be felt more acutely and in many ways because the demand for quality services are projected to grow at a faster rate than before.

2) Lack of teachers, in terms of both quality and quantity. Even in the present scenario, the demand for trained personnel is not met by the existing facilities. With the future growth of tourism at a faster rate, and the greater emphasis on the quality of the training, the capability to meet the demand for human resources will be greatly impaired unless this crucial issue is given the highest attention.

3) Low priority for tourism education and training both by the government and the private sector. The importance of tourism in economic development is now better appreciated. It is also recognised that

proper tourism education can provide a competitive; advantage in this highly competitive market. Yet, training and education are not getting the prominence they deserves, mainly because of the financial constraints that most developing countries face. The result of this unintentional neglect has shown over the years in the cumulative effect on both the quality and content of education. This neglect has manifested generally in a few adverse developments—(a) Numerous educational institutions have mushroomed, taking advantage of the demand for trained manpower. They mostly lack qualified and experienced educators, proper equipment and facilities, (b) These institutions are not , properly monitored and the course contents tend to be diverse and ad-hoc, (c) They also suffer from inadequate linkages with the private sector or with other educational institutions and therefore function in isolation without the benefit of being part of a comprehensive education system.

4) Lack of private sector initiative. The private sector in travel and tourism and hospitality industry is very large but composed of numerous small operators with their fragmented agenda. In fact the apathy of the employers to training is not peculiar to tourism only. The Human Development Report of 2001 pointed out that despite demonstrated gains in productivity from training, employers shy away from training because of a variety of factors like weak management perception, high cost of training, poor information about the benefits of training, inability to exploit the economies of scale in training etc.

5) High cost of training. The future human resource needs are likely to be affected by a few contradictions. In the future, we have seen, the private sector and the employers would need to be more enthusiastic about the training needs of the employees. But the

demands of the new and emerging training requirements and the high costs of such human resource developments are likely to make them less interested than at present. On the other hand in an atmosphere of growing importance of economic liberalisation and privatisation in national economic administration, the governments may expect the industry to take care of the human resource needs of the future. In balance, human resource development, the crucial input of the future tourism development strategy may be the unfortunate victim. High cost of training in the new situation of the future is a fact one can not get away from. However it has to be seen not in isolation but in the overall context of returns to the economy that such training brings. The cost of training is likely to be high because of a variety of factors that have been discussed and can be briefly stated as—

(a) the greater need to ensure the quality of education;

(b) the fast changes in technology related to the tourism industry and the need to adapt to such changes as well as to update the skills from time to time to be in tune with the changes. The employers have to be prepared to be in a permanent training mode' to be in the competitive race;

(c) the complexity of the future training requirements because of the necessity to service an experience to the customer;

(d) the need for comprehensive skill development because the tourism service is to be seen as a total management concept. The need therefore to develop multidisciplinary skills;

(e) tourism services in the future will function in a more interconnected world which has experienced a gap between the supply and demand of the trained personnel in this sector; there will be greater mobility of the personnel and therefore more training costs to the employe

These new developments of a globally mobile labour force and the demands of an interconnected world however raise some very difficult problems. Ten top developed countries of the world today receive more than 50% of the total international tourists arrivals and receipts. In the coming decades this situation is not likely to change much. Therefore the greatest demand for the trained personnel are likely to originate in these countries. Much as the developing countries need human resource developments and the necessary investments that goes with such a policy of development, there is a growing uneasiness that developing country investments in education may subsidise industrial country economies. The Human Development Report of 2001 has pointed out that 100,000 Indian professionals a year are expected to migrate to USA with an estimated resource loss for India of $2 billion. In the tourism education sector this tendency can be reversed by a conscious policy of collaboration across borders, networking among nations to derive economies of scale and by a method of sharing the research findings and innovations with the less developed countries.

**The Way Out**

The problems are such that no simple or single set of solutions can be recommended. The future needs to be constantly under watch and specific remedies to specific situations will have to be found in a collaborative and co-operative endeavour of all concerned. However a few suggestions can be made—

1) **The role of the Government-the State is not dead.** In the overall situation of contradictions where the crucial importance of human resource development is recognised but no one is coming forward to provide

the role of a catalyst, the government should be the leader. In this leadership role, government should provide the symbolic recognition by more budgetary allocations for HRD. It should also be pragmatic in approach to understand that private concerted initiatives will not be forthcoming to the desired extent because of the very nature of the organisation of the tourism industry. The future human resource development will be marked by the quality of the education system. To organise the available private initiatives in the proper direction from the present state of diverse and ad-hoc arrangements, the government should—

a) bring all the tourism educational institutions under a common national umbrella;

b) monitor and co-ordinate the course contents and curricular standards;

c) provide for uniformity in testing and certification system.

There are many instances of the government taking a lead and making a difference in the atmosphere. The initiative of the Singapore government is often quoted for its innovativeness. It extended the university system to link it with the country's industrial policy. Apart from keeping a very tight control over the content and the quality of the courses, it developed a highly effective industrial training system. The government collects 1% of the payroll of employers to subsidize the training of low paid employees under the Skill Development Fund. The Economic Development Board continuously monitors the emerging needs in consultation with the industry and mounts specialised training programmes. The national investment in training was 3.6 per cent of the pay roll in 1995 and was growing. As a result the share of professional and technical workers rose from

15.7% in 1990 to 23.1% in 1995. The Singapore experiment had a few very useful components-raising resources with the collaboration of the private sector, government control over the quality of education, links with the private sector to develop relevant skills and training as a necessary input in the industry on a continuous basis. There are many such experiences around the globe which need to be collated and widely shared.

2) **International co-operation and net-working.** "Building technological capacity in developing countries is central to forging long-term solutions because technologies for development have not, cannot and will not be supplied through the global marketplace alone." (Human Development Report, 2001).

The conference of the tourism professionals organised by ESCAP and WTO referred to earlier, recognised this primary importance of regional and international co-operation to tackle the problems of future HR needs and resolved to "develop regional models of education and training appropriate to various countries, diverse cultures....". If the developing countries are to overcome the problems of high cost of the new training requirements and to gain the advantage of economies of scale, harmonisation of the training needs and contents both internationally and nationally is a primary first task of all concerned.

3) **Widening the reach—training of trainers.** Even with the best of efforts as described, a very large segments of the unorganised sector in tourism which play a very important role in providing the total experience will be left out. PATA was one of the earliest organisations to realise the importance of the training of trainers programme to create a self generating process to facilitate human resource development in countries where educational facilities were deficient.

There were some more initiatives later on from other organisations like the EC but this vital programme has not taken shape as a continues partnership between the public and the private sector.

4) **Collective role of the industry.** Individual and fragmented approach by some industries cannot overcome the constraints that the future efforts for human resource development may face. The travel, tourism and hospitality industry in each country can play a pivotal role by joint efforts. The associations of the private sector must play the role of a catalyst in the interest of its own growth and survival. It can set for itself norms for employment which ensure that tourism education gets a linkage with the industry.

### General: Some Future Concerns

The future human resource development needs cannot be assessed in isolation of the total global development scenario. The world today faces very serious concern of growing prosperity co-existing with increasing poverty and inequality in this world. Since 1980 when the tourism arrivals have almost doubled, sixty countries of the world have been getting steadily poorer. The world Development Report says that in 1820, the start of the modern growth era, the tropical world had a per capita income roughly 70% of that of the temperate world. By 1992 it was just one -quarter.

Tourism, it is said, is the most peaceful weapon of redistribution of income. Tourism can therefore contribute to peace and development if the opportunities offered by the future developments in technology and globalisation are gainfully harnessed by collaborrative initiatives. Along with free movement of goods and services and world-wide spread of knowledge, globalisation and mass tourism also have to contend with trafficking in drugs, human beings and arms, spread of HIV , terrorism and fundamentalism, erosion of ecology and cultural values. All the positive possibilities of tourism will lie in crumpled hopes unless the tourism industry wakes up to the problems and face them together. And there tourism education becomes the key motivator. The Human Development Report points out correctly that at the heart of nurturing creativity is expanding human skills. "For that reason, technological change dramatically raises the premium every country should place on investing in the education and skills of its people." Sound public policy, therefore will make a difference in the way the countries utilise the opportunities.

# 4

# Aviation and Tourism*

It is significant that the major growth in tourism coincided with greater pace of liberalization of the regulatory environment in the global civil aviation scenario.

### Civil Aviation Drives Tourism Growth

Civil Aviation and Tourism have a symbiotic relationship. Each depends on the other for growth and sustenance. Two examples make this relationship amply clear. First is the nature of development of the tourism industry and second, the effects of September 11 events on aviation and its cascading effects on tourism.

It is well known that tourism is the biggest industry of the world today. Even on modest estimate it contributes 3 to 5 per cent of the world GDP. During the last two decades, the international tourism receipts have constantly grown 1.5 times faster than the world GDP. By 1998 international tourism accounted for more than 8 percent of the world's total export earnings and 37 percent of the export in the services sector. With about $ 4 trillion in total output, this industry had surpassed all others by the end of the century and was still growing at a rate faster than the growth of the world econmy.

Fifty years back tourism was hardly noticeable as an industry. In 1950 the arrivals were only 25.3 million and earnings bare $2.1 billion. The phenomenal growth of tourism

---

* Presented in International Conference on Aviation and Tourism Organized by Foundation for Aviation and Sustainable Tourisk (FAST) in New Delhi 11-12 Dec. 2002.

started after 1960. Between 1960 and 1970 the number of arrivals increased two and half times and thereafter till the 90's it has almost doubled every decade. Between 1970 and 2000 the number of arrivals have increased tenfold.

Such remarkable growth was made possible by 9 variety of factors, like the changed safety perception after the end of the Korean War and the Vietnam War, changed geopolitical situations like the break up of the Soviet Union and emergence of the Eastern Europe, economic upturn generally in the world and particularly the rise of the 'Asian Tigers', dismantling of borders and formation of the European Union etc. But perhaps no other factor contributed to this growth more than the growth in the civil aviation sector. This was also the era of unbelievable technological developments in civil aviation. It is no co-incidence that the period of biggest growth in tourism was also the period of introduction of jet propelled, wide-bodied aircrafts making travel faster, quicker and safer. Changes in aviation technology widened the horizon of man's dreams and capabilities to travel. Civil aviation, more than any other factor changed the nature of tourism in the world. And it is predicted that in the future, technological developments in civil aviation will be a major influgnce shaping the trend of tourism developments.

This strong complementary relationship is well illustrated negatively by the effects of the events of 9/11. The immediate psychological impact of he events was to create such fear of flying that by December 2001, US airlines were flying with 40—50 per cent empty seats even after drastically reducing their scheduled flights. The resultant loss to the hotel industry was estimated at $2 billion and the travel agencies were losing an estimated $51 million per day. While everyone is optimistic about the resilience of the industry and expects the 2020 projection of 1.6 billion arrivals to hold good, the year-end review of the WTO does show possible decline in arrivals during the year. "2001 was marked by a loss of consumer confidence and by a feeling of apprehension with regard to travel, especially by air. This was the first crisis in 20 years and the deepest one in the history of international tourism. .....International tourism arrivals were down 0.6 per cent..." It is significant that while long haul destinations suffered most, nearby leisure destinations prospered.

The most telling lesson of this experience has been that anything that affects aviation affects tourism directly. On the other hand the review of experience of national destinations also have shown a few things. First, pragmatic tourism marketing strategies helps revival of the aviation sector. Second, joint public-private and tourism-civil aviation strategies to build consumer confidence prove to be far more effective and productive than isolated efforts by different sectors. Third, many airlines reacted to the fall in demand by short-term strategy of reducing prices, and by long-term structural changes. On both counts, the tourism was the gainer.

### Civil Aviation as a Catalyst for National Tourism Development: An Illustration

That civil aviation, instead of being a service provider only, can also be the change agent for tourism is illustrated by the experience of many countries. The experience of Mexico, which is one of the top ten countries in tourism arrivals, tells the story eloquently. It is a story that may strike many familiar cords in the Indian situation. This story is beautifully related by Mr. Antonio Savignac who was the Planning Minister those days and was also later the Secretary General of the World Tourism Organisation. In the 60s Mexico was desperately looking at various options of strategies for economic developments. The 6 per cent growth rate targeted by them needed the production level to be suitably geared up, which again required larger imports of goods and services. The problem was in finding ways to sustain higher level of imports with higher exports. In their search they found tourism to be an ideal instrument of growth and started taking national initiative for promotion of tourism. After battling with all their problems of co-ordination among various service providers, finally when they were ready to receive the tourists, they were faced with the unexpected problem of not having enough competitive air services. Savignac narrates-"with hotels near completion and almost all infrastructure finally in place and working, and our international and national marketing and promotion programs started, we approached the airlines, both foreign and national, to coordinate their flights and our efforts.

Foreign airlines simply said sorry; your government doesn't allow us to fly to any of your new destinations. It is not covered in our bilateral air agreements.

We talked to our two main national carriers. One, Aeromexico, fully government owned and the other, Mexicana, while privately run, indirectly also majority owned by the government. Their answer: well, yes, since this was a government effort they would supply a few flights a week from Mexico City, as and when and if they had available planes and crews."

The significance of this story is not in its striking similarity to the Indian situation but in the way that Mexico handled it and in the results achieved by them. "The battles were long, hard fought and epic. Accusations were thrown at us as sellers of the country's sovereignty and blue skies." Twenty-five years later, by 1998 they had achieved such synergy between civil aviation and tourism that both grew bigger and better. By this time one newly developed destination -Cancun- had received 2.3 million tourists and earned $1.7 billion. 2.5 million passengers flying into Cancun alone made it the second busiest airport in Mexico and earned for the airlines enough revenue to make them a catalyst in the development process. The Mexico-Europe airfare, just to illustrate, reduced by 44% and there were very few if any limitations on frequencies, or capacity or fares.

A recent assessment by AT Kearney, and quoted by the Ministry of Tourism internally, shows the impact of civil aviation on tourism growth and economic development of

India. It says-"assume on an average: 400 passengers per flight

200 foreign visitors per flight
Stay of seven days
Expenditure of Rs. 2000 per day

Impact: Rs. 28 lakhs foreign exchange earned per flight
Over Rs. 100 crores earned per year (360 Flights)
Over 20,000 jobs created per year.

Just opening up one bilateral slot that Air India is now unable to serve, would create as many jobs as' Air India currently employs."

**The Future Issues and Challenges**

The impact of technological developments is the crucial issue we need to take note of and prepare in time to meet the consequences. In his Somnath Chib memorial lecture in 1999, Lord Marshall then Chairman of British Airways, had pointed to a few issues, which would be important in the future. First, the technology of Hying. 1 he satellite based Future Air Navigation System (FANS) would have the effect of ironing out the world's airways, so that we can fly in straight lines, thus reducing journey time and improving operational efficiency. The industry, it was estimated, would save $10 billion in annual cost saving which would be a great boost at the time that the industry is passing through a tough time. However the nations will have to implement satellite navigation and communication system, which is costly.

Second is the question of technological developments in aircraft manufacturing and further progress in supersonic flights. "We are much more likely to see" he stated " the airframe manufacturers moving on to the concept of mass hypersonic transport outside the earth's atmosphere, turning the trip between Delhi and London into a short-haul experience."

Third, tremendous progress in information technology has empowered the consumer and made him the king. Consumer choices and demands, strengthened by his power given by access through IT today drives the travel and tourism industry and will do so more in the future. Civil aviation infrastructure technology will have to keep in pace with such consumer friendly innovations. For example, smart card with biometric devices for immigration clearance is already available.

The net impact of all such developments, along with factors which propel tourism to grow on its own, is a boom in the traffic. As pointed out by Lord Marshall, by the middle of this decade the annual volume of passenger traffic, which was 1.47 billion in 1998, would have doubled. In 1997 globally, schedule air travel was around 1500 billion. By 2005 this figure is expected to go up to 2700 billion RPMs and by 2015 to 4000 billion RPMs.Even though the events of September 11, have temporarily caused decline in the air traffic, all projections for the future indicate that the industry will bounce back to the expected growth path.

**The Policy Implications**

The implications of such developments are obvious. Any. country, which hopes to be in the race to partake of the great economic opportunities, opened up by travel and tourism must device strategies to provide a totality of services to the consumer in tune with what technology has made possible. Three areas seem to be crucial components of such a strategy. *First,* the air corridors are naturally going to be very congested and crowded. Efficient and safe management of the air space is going to be the primary need of the future. Every country must invest heavily in futuristic technology. Fortunately, access to technology is fairly democratic and easy, but it comes at a cost.

*Second,* as airframe technology is also changing fast, most countries, particularly those, which depend on national carriers, have to invest constantly to acquire the latest technology for passenger comfort and safety.

*Third,* We have to think of totality of services. An efficient flight experience can be totally ruined by inept and inefficient ground handling and services. As the passenger traffic in the world is expected to double and triple within the next few years, the airport terminal facilities, support services, surface access systems, hotel accommodation -all these will have to keep pace. The ideal synergy between civil aviation and tourism implies a situation where the future strategic planning of each sector takes into account the totality of this scenario.

In such a scenario, developing countries like India may find themselves in very serious disadvantage. One major characteristic of the present technological revolution is that technology is changing very fast, and as has been said, each new development compounding the speed and capability of the one that came before it. Acquiring technology becomes more expensive than it was before.

The change in technology also underscores the importance of HRD in any strategic planning for travel and tourism. It goes without saying that it is not the technology as such, but the human capability behind the technology that gives strength to a nation. When technology changes so fast, HRD also becomes a costly proposition. Training has to be continuous and continuously updated. Countries trying hard to find enough resources to provide basic literacy to its population may find it extremely difficult to provide the resources for HRD in travel and tourism.

It was predicted that the process of globalisation, technological developments, and liberalized trading regime would lead to intense competition and ultimately result in change in the organization of travel and tourism business. Global alliances with integrated air services have already become a major pattern of airline business in the world. We have to take note of this development and its implications for the future of our own airlines.

**The Indian Scenario**

The first recorded flight in India was in 1910, just seven

years after the historic flight of the Wright brothers. On October 15,1932 JRD Tate started the civil aviation history of the country by introducing the weekly mail service. The Indian Aircraft Act of 1934 begins the saga of Air India and private initiative in civil aviation. Civil aviation became the first industry to be nationalized when in 1953 by the Air Corporation Act, government nationalized all the airlines.

The Indian scenario is full of many contradictions. Way back in the sixties, when our competitors had not even thought about it, we had the vision of an integrated civil aviation and tourism development strategy. A cabinet rank minister was placed in charge of both the sectors, to enable effective coordination and action. DG Tourism was actively associated in the organisations of Air India and Indian Airlines. Air India in fact was the flag bearer of Indian tourism and even set up a tourism promotion fund in major source markets. Tourism marketing was done jointly and both benefited.

By the time the tourism boom occurred and other countries emulated what we had visualized long back, we had effectively dismantled all these synergies. The resultant lack of coordination affected tourism. For example, hotel infrastructure built in Khajuraho languished for want of adequate flight connectivity. The industry was crying hoarse for long for timely announcement of flight schedules to Ladakh. While government promoted the NE as an integrated circuit, there was no internal connectivity to make it happen. Such problems can be easily taken care of by better and system based coordination.

The great importance of civil aviation for tourism in India is evident from the fact that an estimated 95% of the total international arrivals are by air. On the other hand apparently airlines have not been able to cash on the booming domestic tourism, only 1.2 % of which traveled by air in 1994. After the effects of 9/11 the tourism revival strategy has looked at shorter haul destinations and domestic tourism has been the saviour both for hotel and civil aviation industry.

Civil aviation policy must closely look at tapping this huge potential for development in collaboration with the Ministry of Tourism.

In fact civil aviation has great resources at its disposal that can spread tourism to the far corners of the country. India has more than 120 airports, and another 329 airstrips. China has only 76 airports, which they have managed in such a way that tourism hubs are created to different parts of the country, efficient enough to make China the top destination by 2020. In 1996-97 the top five airports handled 73.5% of the traffic and the rest 115 shared 26.5%. Apparently, spreading out the activities to more airports by creating hubs will generate more traffic, more income and will result in local area development.

Even at the present level of traffic, the infrastructure in the top airports fall short of the world standard. If they are to handle any large inflow the strain will be severe and tourism promotion may be counter productive. The technological vision of the future that we have mentioned earlier would require massive improvements. Many of them can't be brought to the future requirements even with such remodeling. The only alternative is to develop new and modern airports, which will be costly. On a very modest estimate the resource gap of the AAI in the $9^{th}$ Plan was $1429 million. It is inevitable that the strategy should look at more effective public- private partnership as a long-term solution.

The position is made worse by the fact that in 1995-96 only 13 out of 120 airports were profit making. The rest were apparently subsidized by these 13. In overall socio-economic planning there may be some justification for such cross subsidies, but there is also a strong case for commercialization of these airports.

The National Tourism Policy has Avery interesting model about civil aviation and tourism symbiosis. It shows that to accommodate one million additional tourists, Air India will have to invest Rs.10, 530 crores and will earn annually, Rs.l,

936 crores in foreign exchange. This model, the policy says strengthens the argument for opening India's sky for enhancing tourism through increased capacity.

**Needed—Strong Implementation**

Fortunately, all these issues are adequately taken care of in the Draft Civil Aviation policy and the Policy on Airport Infrastructure. Unfortunately, the Draft Policy has been hanging lor the last three years. It is imperative that the good intentions are given shape in a professional manner without any loss of time.

**To Sum Up**

We are living in a world, which is fast changing. Technological revolution makes globalization a reality. Aviation and tourism weaves the global society into a global village. Increasing competitiveness and productivity benefits sweeping the world also marks this world. In such a situation only the best and those who adapt to change survive. Adapt or perish, is the new management mantra of the old Darwinian theory of survival. The most important requirement of progress in this era is willingness and capacity to change the mindset.

For a tourism and aviation strategy, we have to have a comprehensive look at the total journey and totality of the services at the airport and not just at the flight duration, availability of seats etc.

Aviation can play a great role in product development as was shown by the example of Cancun in Mexico. Its strategy should synchronise with the strategy of product development of tourism department.

Civil aviation is passing through a difficult time now, particularly in the South Asia region. It is a time to look at new marketing strategy and at new sources of markets. Joint collaboration in this area will be mutually beneficial.

The huge economic potential of domestic tourism needs to be more closely looked at while finalising the aviation strategy for the future.

*PART II*

# THE PARADISE UNEXPLORED

# 5

# Tourism and Human Resource Development in the North East

This paper is primarily on the theme of opportunities that tourism offers to the NE states and the planning needed to enable the people to take advantage of these opportunities. Tourism itself is a complex phenomenon, involving many activities. It is difficult to get uptodate and reliable data on all the components of tourism activities. Data on the NE are even more difficult to get. The paper therefore mostly relies on data from Assam as a representative sample for the NE. The paper examines the role of human resource development for the tourism sector only.

The presentation is divided into following broad parts:

(I) Why tourism?—A macro view.

1. Issues in tourism human resource development—a global view.
2. Economic development situation in the NE—case study of Assam.
3. Role of tourism in economic development of the NE.
4. Present tourism scenario of the NE.

---

* Paper presented in the National Seminar on "Human Resource Development in the North East in the Era of Globalization" Institute of Applied Manpower Research. New Delhi, 4-5 March 2003.

5. The tourism HRD situation in India.
6. Some broad areas of action for tourism HRD in the NE.

## PART—I

### Why Tourism—A Macro View

Travel is an activity as old as human civilization. But as an important economic activity of the modern age it was hardly noticed even as late as 1950. Thereafter however, it has been a story of remarkable growth. In 1950 a total of 25 million international tourist arrivals generated receipts of $2.1 billion. Thereafter the number of arrivals almost doubled every decade and multiplied ten times during 1970 to 2000 to reach the figure of 700 million arrivals. Between 1970 and 1980 the receipts from tourism increased from $18 billion to $105 billion and has now reached a figure of $500 billion. For the past 15 years the international tourism receipts have grown 1.5 per cent faster than world GDP. By 1994 John Naisbitt in his book, 'Global Paradox', had estimated that tourism with about $3.4 trillion in output was the largest industry in the world. By 1998, the World Tourism Organisation reported that "international tourism accounted for an estimated 8 per cent of the world's total export earnings and 37 per cent of exports in the services sector. International tourism receipts and passenger transport amounted to more than $504 billion, putting it ahead of all other categories of international trade as shown below—

| | *Category of trade* | *$ billion* |
|---|---|---|
| 1. | International tourism | 504 |
| 2. | Automotive products | 496 |
| 3. | Chemicals | 490 |
| 4. | Food | 458 |
| 5. | Petroleum and other fuels | 435 |
| 6. | Computers and office equipment | 394 |
| 7. | Textiles and clothing | 332 |

| | | |
|---|---|---|
| 8. | Telecommunications equipment | 279 |
| 9. | Mining products | 163 |
| 10. | Iron and steel | 141 |

At the beginning of the 21st Century, tourism's great contribution to economic development has been widely accepted. Even a modest estimate by the WTO shows that tourism contributes 3-5 per cent of the world GDP. It is one of the 5 top export items of 83 per cent countries of the world and it is the main source of foreign exchange earnings of at least 38 per cent countries of the world. It employs about 11 per cent of the direct employment of the world. The World Travel and Tourism Council (WTTC) however thinks that the contributions of tourism 'economy' is much bigger, and in fact, commonly states that every 5 seconds some travel and tourism related job is created around the world.

**Tourism: A Multidimensional Activity**

The actual impact of tourism will be apparent only when the multidimensional nature of tourism is understood. It is essential, when planning for human resource development, to take into account all the sectors where tourism can have impact. The difficulties arise, as pointed out by the 'Economist' in 'Survey of World Travel and Tourism' scenario in 1993, on three counts.

First, there is no clear definition of what constitutes tourism. Tourism involves many activities, the content and import of which change from country-to-country. Therefore, a common denominator is difficult to find. The WTTC has identified more than 30 activities to be at the 'core' of tourism business in any country. In common practice, while talking of tourism, reference is made only to about four or five of them, namely, accommodation, travel, transport and entertainment. But the 'ripple' effect of tourism flows through the economy covering a host of other activities. (Annexure 1). The WTTC therefore distinguishes between 'T&T Industry' and 'T&T Economy'. Travel and Tourism Industry includes those activities traditionally associated with travel and tourism like transport, accommodation and catering. Travel and tourism economy includes the impact of travel and tourism and its flow-through effect across the wider economy. It is a vital difference and should be kept in mind while assessing the economic importance of tourism in development planning.

Second, many of these activities cannot be easily quantified and therefore tend to be left out of accounting.

Third, international comparison is "bedevilled" says the Economist, "by astounding differences" in the method of data collecting and interpretation. This is a serious problem of accounting in India and more so in the NE states, for which the contribution of tourism tend to be underestimated or remain as 'invisible'.

**Factors That Helped This 'Boom'**

While planning for the future of tourism, it is necessary to understand the factors which made this growth possible and also to take into account the influences which are likely to shape the future growth.

Foremost among the factors which pushed tourism to such a prominent economic activity was the revolution in the aviation technology. The introduction of jet propelled wide-bodied aircraft made travel easier, faster and less bothersome. The world economic growth was fairly steady during this period and it improved the capability of the prospective traveller by placing more disposable income at his command. The East Asian economic miracle, despite the occasional hiccups, was an important factor in this growth because, the Asia Pacific region has emerged as the fastest growing region both for inbound as well as outbound tourism.

The geo-political situation in the world during the last fifty years also changed beyond all recognition—changes, which were in general, conducive to the growth of tourism. The end of the Vietnam War and the Korean War improved perception about the safety of travel. Korea has recorded fast growth in tourism and Vietnam is emerging as a prominent destination in Asia Pacific. The end of the cold war furthered strengthened the travel atmosphere. The breaking up of the Soviet Union and political changes in Eastern Europe and subsequent economic liberalization measures have added 430 million people of these countries—larger than the population of Western Europe—to the category of potential travellers.

The last two decades of the century have seen tremendous changes in Asia as well. Economic liberalization measures in China and India, which account for more than 38 per cent of the world's population, is already showing impact on tourism. India's outbound tourists of about 4 million is growing faster than the inbound. According to the WTO China is projected to generate 100 million—the highest in the world—tourists by 2020.

The process of globalisation has further strengthened the growth of tourism, moving towards the concept of a global village. The dismantling of borders in Europe, emergence of more and more free trade zones, more regional alliances in trade and commerce and tourism, growing liberalization of visa formalities adopted by increasing number of countries are some of the other developments that give a boost to the indomitable roving spirit of the human beings.

### The Future Scenario—Will 9/11 and 'War Clouds' Change it All?

Before the new millennium was ushered in, enthused by all these developments, the WTO had made a 2020 vision projection. It had projected a staggering 1.6 billion international arrivals and $2000 billion in tourism receipts alone. The brief projections relating to India are shown below—

| | *2010* | *2020* |
|---|---|---|
| World | 1000 m | 1561 m |
| South Asia | 11 m | 19 m |
| India | 5.1 m | 8.9 m |

As the WTO points out international tourism is still in its 'infancy.' Only 7 per cent of the total population of the world who are capable of travelling are actually travelling now. There is therefore great latent capacity.

The 9/11 events created such fear of flying immediately that as a consequence the industry faced 'the deepest crisis in the history of world tourism' according to the WTO. In USA airlines were flying with 40/50 per cent empty seats, many airlines had to wind up business and in the short run, hotels were losing $51 m a day. By the end of 2001, however, there was cautious optimism and the figures also showed hope—

| | *World* | *South Asia* | *East Asia Pacific* | *Africa* |
|---|---|---|---|---|
| Oct. Dec. 2001 | (–8.6) | (–24.4) | (–4.2) | (–1.4) |
| 2001 | (–0.6) | (–6.3) | (5.5) | (4.4) |

By the end of 2002 the growth rate of world tourism achieved a figure of 3.1 per cent—a shade lower than the projected but nevertheless a reassuring turn around.The industry is now convinced of the resilience of the sector as shown by the recovery after the earlier crisis like the Gulf War, the Kosovo conflict, events in Egypt and terrorist acts in Sri Lanka. The WTO has not altered its projection for 2020.

Tourism is very price sensitive and depends more on economic growth than anything else. The world recovery process has been slow, all the economic indicators started on a false note. By the beginning of 2003 Oil prices had shot up to $30 a barrel, gold prices were up and the stock exchanges were down in important places. War clouds still threaten the horizon and may deter the traveller from taking a long haul flight.

However, there are lessons to be learnt. The aggregates may inspire hope, but they conceal wide regional differences. War in the region, or even a threat of it may slow down the recovery process. The future strategic planning must take into account the many implications of this experience, like looking for new short haul destinations, and new marketing strategies. For the NE, few aspects are most relevant. First, government must play a positive role to integrate tourism planning with general economic planning. Second, a strong public private partnership must be developed to provide fillip to private initiative. Third, and the most important, domestic tourism which is booming and growing at a very fast pace should be the cornerstone of tourism planning. Domestic tourism can be particularly relevant for the NE states which suffer from communication disadvantage and image problems.

### The Future Challenges

There is general agreement that the most definite influences to shape the future of tourism can be grouped into the following:

1. Socio-demographic factors;
2. Technological revolution;
3. Changes in consumer behaviour;
4. Concern for sustainable development;
5. Human resource development.

The ability of any country to incorporate the nuances of these influences into the strategies for tourism promotion would decide its competitiveness in the global scenario. Each of these influences would be crucial, but the most important, as noted by the then Deputy Secretary General of the WTO Mr. Frangialli in his Somnath Chib memorial lecture in 1994, "human resources could emerge as the single most important issue facing tourism operation into the next century."

### HRD—A Global View

It is commonly said that tourism has made the world a global village. The process of globalisation has changed the pattern of travel and tourism industry and the manner of doing business. The process of international economic liberalization and technological developments have made it possible for tourism business to go beyond the national borders.

Expectations of tourists about the quality of service have also increased.

## PART—II

### Economic Situation in the NE—Some Salient Features

The NE is a geographically homogeneous area but with wide diversity. Generalisation of the economic situation of the area therefore may be inaccurate. Economic situation also covers important issues of infrastructure development, productivity, sectoral balances, investment opportunities and income and employment generation measures—issues which constantly receive the attention of policy makers at the highest level in the country. Equally important are the socio-political issues which are crucial parameters to be taken into account while planning economic development strategies. In this section we examine only those feature which have direct bearing on the thesis that tourism can play an important role in the economic development planning of the region.

#### *1. General Deceleration in the Economy*

The most striking feature of the economic development of the region has been a general downturn in economic performance compared to other states in the last few decades. It is reflected in the rate and pattern of growth of Net State Domestic Products (NSDP) and per capita income of the population. Dr. Gulshan Sachdeva in a paper ('North-Eastern Economy: Past Policies, Present Realities and Future Possibilities) presented in a Seminar on "North-East: Challenges and Response" (Nehru Memorial Museum, Teen Murti House, New Delhi, 19-21 December 2002) points out that "while the national economy is growing fast after initial contraction, the economies of the region are slowing down. In the decade of eighties growth rates in the North-Eastern Region were lower than the national growth rates. In the last few years the gap between national growth and regional growth rates has further widened."

However some of the states showed higher growth rates

during this period. Dr. Jayant Madhab ('Commentary on the Fiscal Situation of the North Eastern States' Dialogue, Vol.-4 No. 1) points out that this was mostly due to higher construction (mainly roads) activities financed by the Central Government in certain years. The most disturbing is the performance of the biggest economy in the region—Assam. At the time of Independence and the beginning of planned development in the country, Assam's per capita income was 4 per cent higher than the national at constant prices. By 1998-99 it was 41 per cent below the national average at current prices and 45 per cent below at 1980-81 prices. "What is even more alarming," states the Assam Development Report (Planning Commission) "is that the gap is growing. Between 1980 and 1990, per capita income at 1980-81 prices grew by 20 per cent in Assam compared with 40 per cent for all-India. Between 1980 and 1998 per capita income in Assam grew by 10 per cent compared with 39 per cent for all India.......Assam's economy decelerated in the 1990s." It is very significant that this was the period of good growth for most states spurred by economic liberalization measures.

### 2. *Higher Unemployment and Poverty*

Naturally, the stagnation in economic activities shows in fallout on human development indicators. For almost all the states the percentage of people below poverty line is substantially higher than the national average. The unemployment figures also show most states to be above the national average—Assam again being alarmingly high. One further estimate quoted by Shri H.N Das (Dialogue, volume 4 no. 1) shows that the percentage of unemployment among he youths of 15-29 age group has increased in Assam from 3.01 in 1983-84 to 19.25 in 1993-94 against the all India figure of 6.46 per cent that year.

### 3. *Distorted Sectoral Growth*

Neither industry nor agriculture has grown, as is to be expected. In Assam for example, in the 1990s the growth rate of agriculture slowed down to 1.6 per cent from the low figure of 2.1 of the earlier decade. Lower productivity of these sectors is compounded by disproportionate growth of the service sector. Dr. P.R. Bhattacharjee ('The problem of Ensuring Financial Efficiency in the North –Eastern States' Dialogue, volume 4 no. 1) shows that the tertiary sector has become unduly inflated owing to the tendency of the states to find employment in the public sector to accommodate the growing unemployed. This has led to lower productivity of investment leading further to lower income generation, resulting in lower expenditure in capital and development areas and therefore a continuing vicious cycle of underdevelopment. The resulting fiscal mismatch has found most of the states in serious financial distress and debt servicing has become one of the biggest component of the state expenditure. It increased from Rs. 733.34 crore in 1980 to Rs. 11,351.39 crore in 2001 in Assam and the fresh borrowing was almost eaten up by the interest payments. The Committee on Fiscal Reform set up by the Government of Assam pointed out that "out of a total amount of Rs. 4977.62 crore of unearmarked fund in Assam's 9th Five Year Plan as much as Rs. 4112.76 crore will be spent on salaries and establishment, constituting 82.62 per cent." The fact that 48.41 per cent of the earmarked fund also is spent on salaries and establishment should cause serious concern.

**4. *'Unbalanced Economy'***

Prof. Sachdeva has pointed out that the states oft the region import food items worth about Rs. 2000 to 2500 crore annually. That a primarily agrarian and predominantly rural economy of the region should depend so heavily on the outside for primary food items reflects the weakness of the economic planning strategy. This weakness is further compounded by the fact that most of the export items of the region are primary resource based products like tea, petroleum products, plywood etc.

**5. *Quality in Human Resource Development***

The region has fairly high levels of literacy rates. Some

states like Mizoram are way above the national average, but except Arunachal Pradesh all other states are at the national level or higher. Yet, the number of trained teacher is only 45 per cent against the national average of 87 per cent. Prof Sachdeva has quoted figures to show that in Assam and Nagaland only about 30 per cent of the higher secondary teachers are trained. Quality in human resource development should therefore be a major plank of economic development strategy.

**What is the Way Out?**

The future strategy naturally will have to be multi-pronged and extensive. However any strategy must address the core malaise—lack of additional income and employment generating activities. The essential element of a strategy would be to focus on sectors that have high employment, income and output generating capabilities and have strong backward and forward inter-sectoral linkages.

The Assam Development Report commenting on the situation in Assam recommends that "priority should be given to those sectors, which have both comparative advantage and high linkages with other sectors." This prescription should be valid for the entire NE as well. Because of its geographical isolation and distance from the market and sources of raw materials, investment on the locally available resources would be most cost effective.

As we have seen, the states of the region have very precarious financial strength and private investment that can create additional income and employment are also negligible because of a variety of reasons. In such a situation the investment portfolio should compose of projects which require the least government investment and which have the highest multiplier effect on income and employment. Investments which have higher dispersal effects and are not concentrated in pockets would be ideal to provide the much needed push to the economy.

## Tourism—A Key Component of the Solution

Tourism fits this bill perfectly. However, it is essential to remember that tourism should not be projected as 'the' solution but as one of the important inputs to a solution. The Assam Development Report rightly projects tourism as one of the sectors that can kick start the development process.

The economic impact of tourism are well-known and have been well documented. However a case study of Mexico—a country now in the top ten group of international tourism—lucidly narrated by its former Minister in his National Tourism Day lecture in New Delhi succinctly puts across the many facets of tourism.

## "The Story Begins in the Mid-60s...

The aim of the government was to achieve a 6 per cent average annual real rate of growth of the Gross Domestic Product (GDP), while maintaining a low level of inflation. The reason—to absorb an increase of population then about 3.5 per cent annually, and to provide 2.5 per cent for growth and social improvement.

The problem. 6 per cent growth meant an increase in production; increase in production meant increase in imports...increase in imports meant obtaining more foreign currency,...to pay for increased imports....

The search: an exhaustive on going analysis was made of all types of goods and services that could be exported: agriculture, fisheries, mining, manufactured and semi-manufactured goods, etc. All types of assumptions, combinations and projections were run through....

However, one of the curious activities that continually kept appearing was the case of tourism. Tourism to Mexico had been growing consistently and successfully in various destinations without any planning , fiscal incentives or credit facilities and despite whole series of red tape and lack of facilitation.

A strange beast that seemed to grow like a weed, with no fertilizer, irrigation, care or attention.

Knowing nothing about this activity we promptly set out to analyze it....

Our conclusions were surprising at least to us, who were novices in this field:

1. It could be developed and promoted almost anywhere.
2. It grew with little if any, government help, programmes or policies.
3. It offered an infinity of products and possibilities such as business, conventions, cruise, nature (parks, lakes, mountains) archaelogy, cities, sports, adventure, sun and beaches, culture, folklore, music, astronomy and so forth.
4. It was relatively free of restrictions, unlike other exports of goods and commodities which were subject to quotas, taxes, import permits and many others.
5. Generally it did not consume non-renewable resources, nor did it involve dangerous processes.
6. It was labour intensive and, being a personal service, hard to automate or replace.
7. The technology for its development was well-known and easily available....
8. Training of personnel was generally easy, available and quick...
9. Foreign tourism was capable of providing an ever increasing flow of foreign currency.
10. The foreign import component of the industry was exceptionally low....It was estimated to be only 6 to 8 of the total investments, as compared to 35 to 45 per cent of the automobile industry. This meant most

of the investments and expenditures would remain in the country, with little foreign currency impact.

11. The expenditure by foreign and national tourists would be spread over a wide variety of business, big and small. For example, excluding air transport, for every 100 units spent in the country the breakdown was estimated to be:

| | | | |
|---|---|---|---|
| Lodging | — | 30-35 | per cent |
| Food and beverages | — | 20-25 | per cent |
| Handicrafts | — | 10-15 | per cent |
| Local transportation | — | 10 | per cent |
| Shopping, guides, entertainment etc. | — | 20-25 | per cent |

12. The tourist expenditure within the country is almost always equivalent to cash.... This means immediate cash flow as compared to financing of conventional export products.

We were amazed to find this hidden and, to us, unknown jewel but our biggest surprise, what really made it unique, was the way the product is consumed.

How so? Well, traditionally products, be they industrial...or agricultural..., consumer goods..., or others, regardless of where they are produced, must be shipped and delivered for their use or consumption where the purchaser or client resides.

This means packaging, transporting, distributing and servicing the product,....

Tourism in this respect is unique because the consumer must displace himself along with his money, to his destination be it for... any of the myriad tourism products.

This makes tourism an incredibly agile and flexible tool for economic and social development...agriculture can be developed and is limited in its scope to the availability of sun, water, and climate among others. Mining can be developed where the resource is found. Industry tends to concentrate in or near the large centers of consumption, where it finds the needed infrastructure, energy, technicians, suppliers etc.

Tourism, on the other hand, given its enormous variety of segments, for all tastes and budgets, can truly be developed almost anywhere there is something of interest to do or enjoy.

To make a longer story slightly shorter, the Mexican Government concluded that if tourism had grown so well and so consistently, with little, if any, encouragement what it would not do with some help and support in planning, financing, promotion, facilitation and political and budgetary backing."

The rest is now history. This story could be very relevant for the NE placed in a similar situation of economic and financial doldrums that Mexico was then, because, it has the comparative advantage in natural beauty, fauna, flora, colourful mosaic of ethnicity, history and archaeology that can create the 'unique experience' that the modern tourist is looking for.

That the benefits of employment and income generation through tourism can be quite substantial for the NE is illustrated by the experience at the national level. Rough official estimates of the multiplier effects of tourism in employment creation shows that it is a high figure of 1:1.6. Tourism contributes direct employment of about 2.4 per cent of the workforce. In 2001 tourism sector was estimated to have provided direct employment of 17 million and indirect employment of 25 million. Considering the inadequacies of the accounting system as already indicated, these estimates could be quite on the lower side. The Planning Commission's report on Targeting Ten Million Employment Opportunities per year projects a figure of 3.6 million jobs per year in this sector alone.

The pre-eminence of this sector in employment generation is amply illustrated by a sample survey conducted by the

Ministry of Tourism. It showed that for every million rupees invested at 1985-86 prices, the employment potential of different sectors are as follows:

| *Sector* | *Jobs* |
|---|---|
| Agriculture | 44.7 |
| Manufacturing | 12.6 |
| Mining and quarrying | 2.6 |
| Railways | 0.9 |
| Other transport | 13.8 |
| Tourism | 47.5 |
| (Hotels and Restaurants) | 89.0 |

According to the WTTC the total impact of tourism in the economy is perhaps much bigger and could be still larger in the future if proper policies are followed. Following the concept of travel and tourism economy, which tries to capture the full impact of tourism through all the related activities, it shows that the present and future contribution are:

| *T&T Economy* | *1998* | *2010* |
|---|---|---|
| GDP | 5.6% | 6.6% |
| Employment | 5.8% | 6.8% |

During this period an additional 8 million jobs could be created in tourism related activities, accounting for 1 in every 15 jobs in India. In concrete terms the illustrative increases could be as follows:

| | *1998* | *2010* |
|---|---|---|
| GDP (T&T) | Rs. 90,400 crore | Rs. 5,00,000 crore |
| Capital Investment | Rs. 24,800 crore | Rs. 1,30,000 crore |
| Exports | Rs. 23,100 crore | Rs. 1,60,000 crore |

The WTTC recommends the following basic steps as necessary condition to achieve these potential—

1. An integrated strategy involving the private sector;
2. Strong, sustained policy implementation driven from the top;

3. Progressive liberalization—particularly of aviation;
4. Removing barriers to growth and private initiatives;
5. Investment in infrastructure and human resource development.

There are many intangible benefits of tourism like its contribution to national harmony and understanding, preservation of culture and heritage etc. which don't get quantified in these accounting systems. A sample survey by the Ministry of Tourism has found some very interesting impact of tourism on the local artists and craftsmen, "the study indicates that about 96 per cent of total income of he artisan household in Kerala and about 90 per cent in Rajasthan comes from the tourism related artisan income. Exposure to tourism activities enhances the scope of employment generation, particularly in the lower income segment of the artisan household....As regards Folk Artists their average per capita income during the peak tourist season is nearly four times that in lean season in both the states."('Tourist Statistics' Ministry of Tourism, Government of India.)

### NE Tourism—A Dismal Picture

The present status of tourism in the NE is nowhere near its potential. The arrival figure, both domestic and international, are insignificant.

| | *1999* | *2000* | *2001* | *2005* |
|---|---|---|---|---|
| Arunachal Pradesh | 1008/48 | 9932/2044 | 6349/ 323 | 305/289 |
| Assam | 14336/604 | 891433/5954 | 1010651/6171 | 2467652/10782 |
| Manipur | 97523/277 | 105167/429 | 76527/183 | 94299/316 |
| Meghalaya | 159730/1971 | 169929/2327 | 178697/2390 | 375901/5099 |
| Mizoram | 27139/216 | 28221/235 | 28771/152 | 44715/273 |
| Nagaland | 21041/119 | 13272/451 | 9946/920 | 17470/883 |
| Sikkim | 138785/8554 | 143105/10409 | 203306/31028 | 151744/16523 |
| Tripura | 246507/335 | 231902/0 | 254912/0 | 216330/2677 |
| *All India* | *190671014/5832105* | *22106941/5893542* | *234200935/5427366* | *390466880/9939782* |

*Source:* Tourist Statistics 2005 Ministry of Tourism Government of India.
(The first figures are for domestic and the second for international).

The total number of approved hotels and the room capacity as shown below also shows the poor state of infrastructure.

*(2005)*

| | *No. of approved hotels* | *No. of rooms* |
|---|---|---|
| Arunachal Pradesh | | |
| Assam | 4 | 272 |
| Manipur | — | — |
| Meghalaya | 1 | 50 |
| Mizoram | 1 | 28 |
| Nagaland | | |
| Tripura | | |
| Sikkim | 1 | 28 |

It is apparent that the hospitality sector is predominantly is in the unapproved and unorganized sector. Therefore, the need for improvement in quality and training to achieve quality is even more important.

The NE, with its intrinsic tourism potential and comparative advantage could partake of similar benefits from tourism if similar policy decisions are taken. As a first step, broadly, it will be necessary to adopt a pragmatic tourism policy within which should be a strategy for coordinated human resource development.

**Elements of a Tourism Initiative for the NE**

The first requirement of any initiative on tourism is to chart out the directions of action, and to set the policy about tourism clearly. Because of the very nature of the tourism activity the impact as we have shown, tends to remain invisible. In spite of its potential and relevance tourism is not a high priority either in the thinking or in terms of resource allocation in the NE. Every state must therefore adopt a pragmatic tourism policy wherein the role of each of the major players—the Government, the private sector, the people—are clearly spelt out.

The policy should aim to achieve integration at three levels—(a) integration within the NE states; (b) integration in each state among the different players; (c) integration with the national level stakeholders who play an important role in the process.

For getting the best advantage, tourism planning in the NE whether aimed at domestic or foreign tourists, must be based on an integrated NE perspective. The strength of each should complement each other rather than competing with each other. Unfortunately this extremely vital necessity of projecting the totality of NE suffers from two fundamental inadequacies—

1. Internal communication between the NE states is almost non-existent. Coordinated tourism is possible only when quick air communication between the states is established. Fortunately, aviation infrastructure is already available in all the states and the Indian Airlines have already announced a connectivity network for the NE. Combined action of the industry and the governments of the region must ensure that this planning is translated into action.
2. There is no organizational set up for harmonious action for projecting NE as a whole. If tourism in the NE has to grow a common platform for coordination, involving the governments, the non-governmental agencies and the industry should be immediately be set up.

Even within the state, tourism policy often remains as the wish list of the department of tourism. Tourism being a multidimensional activity, its success depends on the active involvement of the other players. Tourism policy should therefore be integrated into the total development planning of the state and the role of each department should be clearly spelt out.

The problems of civil aviation for example, highlights

the need for close collaboration with national level agencies whose action have impact on the planning of the states. Quite often speedy action in the states are stalled, may be for justified reasons, if the regulating Ministries like Environment, Home, Culture etc. have a different viewpoint. A mechanism for speedy resolution of such differences in respect of NE should be a part of the tourism development strategy.

For the NE whose most valuable assets are the natural eco-systems, preservation of the natural resources through a sustainable tourism practices should be at the core of the tourism policy. Rapid growth of tourism unless properly guided and managed, may lead to slow degradation of the environment. For the local people the temptation of quick economic gains from tourism is too strong to resist and future concerns may not be very understandable. The problem has to be tackled on many fronts—social, economical and psychological. There are numerous examples of unmindful pursuit of tourism leading to unsustainable practices, degradation of the eco-system, cultural degeneration, and changing life style of the local people. Happily, there are also many examples of how determined steps taken by the government and the people can revive dying art and craft, improve the environment, and provide income to the host community through tourism. However, government has to play a very strong regulatory role. First, suitable legal and institutional framework should be devised to protect the larger interest of the community. Second, and equally important, is the need to take positive steps to provide alternative economic means through tourism, to the people who would otherwise resort to unsustainable practices for their present survival.

Even though there are plenty of regulations for the preservation and control of the environment both at the state level and at the centre, many of them have become quite obsolete and irrelevant. Many of them do not address the emerging problems of the present day nor do they offer modern solutions. In most case implementation is slack and often they are implemented in isolation, often too rigidly by the controlling department without proper appreciation of the spin off problems created for other sectors. Government should therefore put in place a set of pragmatic legislations which are in tune with the general government policy, and which can be easily implemented. In particular the states and the center should—

(a) Make an inventory of all the existing legislations on environmental issues;

(b) Weed out the obsolete ones;

(c) Frame new legislations which cover areas hitherto uncovered and reflect regional variations and avoid stereotype rigidity in implementation;

(d) Ensure strict implementation;

(e) For most effective implementation, public support should be enlisted by setting up monitoring mechanism involving the public.

Participatory implementation is the only solution to the problem of environmental protection and departmental coordination is the basic requirement for its success.

The bane of modern development in the ecologically fragile NE has been the very destructive construction practices. Tourism development has also contributed to this malaise. Construction in the tourism sector should be aesthetically pleasant, based on local skill, blend with the surroundings, use local resources and should be functionally efficient. Government should adopt a suitable architectural Code and make it obligatory, as has been done in many parts of the world, to conform to the basic ground rules.

The state of infrastructure development in the NE would require a lot of attention if tourism has to grow at a fast rate and has to become competitive. In the context of very precarious financial position of most of the states, lack of resources may sap any new initiative on the tourism sector. For example, the Assam Development Report has assessed that to achieve a growth rate of 6 per cent in the economy the quantum of investment required in the Trade, Hotels and Restaurants sector would be around Rs. 7,984 crore for the next five years. As such levels of investment are not available, the normal reaction would be to forget about the idea. However, pragmatic thinking may find possible solutions to the problems of resources. In this connection, a comprehensive approach involving the following guidelines are suggested—

(a) *Prioritise—A selective approach to investment.* In our system of democratic governance, there is a tendency to take up too many schemes in a routine unimaginative manner. As a result the investments fail to have any visible impact. Instead, it is suggested that the source of investment funding and the quantum should depend on the relative importance of the project from the point of view of tourists. The tourists could be classified into three categories—international, domestic, i.e., Indian tourists but from outside the region and local and regional i.e. those who are from the area. The tourism products should be identified and classified according to their importance related to each category. Every district should draw up a bench-mark survey of tourism products and attractions. Thereafter, those which primarily satisfy local demands should be included in the district development plans. The regional attractions should be taken care of by the state plan schemes and national and internationally important ones should be taken up with the assistance of the national government and international agencies.

(b) *Tourism focus in other departmental schemes.* A tourism product cannot be developed by the tourism department alone. Other departments like forest, roads, culture can play a very important role in developing a total tourism product. States like Rajasthan and Kerala have reaped great benefits by adopting a general government policy to give relative priority to tourism components in other department's schemes. In this way, greater resources become available for tourism infrastructure.

(c) *Building public private partnership.* Tourism is primarily a private sector driven industry. All over the world, countries which have been successful in tourism have devised policies for strong partnership between the private and the public sectors. States like Kerala and Rajasthan which are leading in tourism in the country have benefited from a strong partnership. Private initiative in the tourism sector in the NE has been negligible. The NE suffers from many inherent infrastructural weaknesses hindering private sector growth. The state governments must therefore come out with very comprehensive and competitive incentive and assistance policies for the private sector on the tourism industry. It will in the long run ease the financial burden of the government for infrastructure development.

(d) *People's participation.* People should be at the core of any tourism business. People's participation and involvement in developing the tourism product may, apart from other benefits, help in local resource mobilization.

As is evident from the tourism statistics for the region, NE also has missed out on the great boom in domestic tourism which has now reached 230 million. The flow of domestic tourists should start the process of awareness creation and development of infrastructure that is needed to attract tourists. More important, it will slowly erase from public mind the stigma of the image of a difficult place now attached to the NE. Tourism and peace has a symbiotic relationship aptly summed up in the famous quote of Gandhiji,"travel is the language of peace."

**Human Resource Development in Tourism—The Key**

The tourism scenario, both national and international holds great promise as already shown but the future will also be of immense competition. HRD will be the tool to give competitive edge because tourism is about providing service. The future travellers are likely to be more demanding of excellence in services. Every country is now competing with each other to provide a totality of services and packaging of product in such a way as to create a 'unique experience' for the visitor. Mr. Tom Baum ('Human Resources in Tourism:An Introduction' in Human Resource Issues in International Tourism) points out that the tourists are not just statistics but are people, whose behaviour, demand, and decision making and response cannot be totally predicted. The tourism product is dependent for its delivery on the human factor. Many tourism products actually include people as an integral part of the tourism experience.

The very fact that the human factor is so important in tourism makes HRD planning imperative but very difficult. First, because of the very nature of tourism, the field of employment is diverse. There is no single center of production. It is a consumer activity which has wide ripple effect on wide range of industries. Most often the range of planning for tourism human resource tend to be confined to the few activities that are most visible, like the hospitality sector and the travel and tourism business. But as the National Tourism Committee Report (1988) has pointed out areas of training should be much larger.

Failure to take a macro view of the human resources required across all sectors of the economy where tourism activity has impact, is a problem faced by the tourism planners. The range of jobs differ widely in terms of technical demands, educational requirements, location etc. In planning institutions and the curriculum for the future this aspect should be kept in view and a coordinated view of HRD should be taken.

The other important aspect in planning is to appreciate

that effective HRD planning takes time. Because it has a lead time, it has to be planned well ahead of the general planning for tourism development. Unless the planners have a futuristic view and can anticipate the growth of tourism, this mismatch may have adverse effects on tourism development itself. An effective HRD planning for the NE should precede the actual implementation of the tourism product development strategies.

### HRD—The Indian Scenario

Fortunately, there is a strong network of HRD institutions in the country but it has primarily remained the responsibility of the government. Starting with 1982, the Government of India has set up a range of institutions offering different levels of training—degree, diploma and certificate apart from programmes of training of trainers from time to time. There are altogether 33 training institutions in the public sector in hospitality management and allied crafts In addition there are the national institutes in travel and tourism, water sports, and hospitality and catering.

The gap between demand and supply and the present position of HRD education in the country is shown in the Draft Report of the Working Group on Tourism for the 10th Five Year Plan. There are about 30 universities running Tourism courses at the Post graduate level and at least 50 colleges of University Grants Commission conduct tourism as a subject at the degree level. The training inputs are equally distributed between the government colleges (47 per cent) and unaided private institutions.(44 per cent). But the percentage of trained managers to total employment was reported to be only 2.58 per cent.

It is estimated that more than 50 per cent of total employment generated by tourism industry is provided by hotel and catering sector. But there is a big gap between demand and supply in the sector. An internal survey conducted by the National Council for Hotel Management of additional manpower that would be required in the industry (surveying only 9 sectors) for the next five years shows—

| *2000-01* | *2001-02* | *2002-03* | *2003-04* | *2004-05* |
|---|---|---|---|---|
| 49,866 | 42,958 | 41,427 | 41,736 | 36,549 |
| % of supply of trained manpower at current rate | | | | |
| 22.5% | 26.19% | 26.0% | 26.0% | 50.50% |

The survey also indicates the pattern of employment in different segments—

| | | | |
|---|---|---|---|
| 1. | Hotels | — | 55 per cent |
| 2. | Restaurants | — | 12 per cent |
| 3. | Airlines, Shipping and Railways | — | 13 per cent |
| 4. | Industrial canteens | — | 10 per cent |
| 5. | Hospitals | — | 3 per cent |
| 6. | Self-employment/Teaching | — | 7 per cent |

Against the requirement shown above the total training capacity currently available are—

| | |
|---|---|
| Government sector | 5680 |
| Private sector | 4390 |
| Apprenticeship scheme | 1600 |
| Total | 11670 |

Thus even a limited survey of two segments of the industry at the present level of international arrivals which is much below the capabilities of the country, shows the need for wide ranging steps to increase the scope of HRD in tourism. This need will increase with the growth of tourists arrivals. The Ministry of Tourism estimates that manpower requirement in the hospitality sector is a function of tourist arrivals. According to this assessment , 2.64 foreign tourist arrivals creates one man year of employment and 37.43 domestic tourist generates one man year of employment.

**Future Tourism HRD for the NE—Some Thoughts**

1. The strategy for HRD in the NE will depend on the role and priority assigned by the governments in the

coming years. HRD planning will have to be synchronized with the planning of tourism infrastructure so that there is no lag between the two.

2. There are only two institutions at the government level on hospitality and tourism in the entire NE. At the present state of tourism in the region they may be sufficient to sustain the need. There is hardly any private sector institution catering to tourism education. As tourism grows as it should, the need for more institutions will be felt. Naturally in such a planning the private sector should be an active partner. But the essential part of the strategy will be to start the planning now.
3. As we have seen, most often, HRD education and training in the tourism sector are confined to a few segments of the industry. It is not necessary to take such a restrictive view of the matter. In the future, successful programmes must integrate with the wider segments of the industry to provide full benefits of employment to the region.
4. Partnership with the private sector should be transparent and integrated. In particular—
   (a) Incentives to be provided to the private sector to overcome the inherent and comparative difficulties of investment in the region.
   (b) They could be involved in cost sharing of HRD schemes, on the basis of benefits that accrue, in the Singapore pattern.
   (c) The industry must be involved in designing the course contents, so that they are relevant to the industry. They should provide practical training facilities as well as be part of the faculty in some suitable arrangements.
   (d) As a corollary of such involvement, employment

of trained personnel in the private sector should be made a voluntary obligation.

5. The human resource development strategy should be in different stages. In the first stage the focus should be on meeting the basic needs of the trade. In the second stage, specialized training to upgrade the skill and to train total managers to provide the service that can create the experience we have talked about should be put in place.
6. There is a very large unorganized segment in the tourism and hospitality industry which does not come under any regulation of the government or of the industry organisations. Even in the regulated segments, there is need for continuous training in this age of fast changing techniques. A well designed 'training of trainers' scheme should be introduced to cover this gap in training with least cost to the small and urorganised establishments.

The NE has tremendous potential for tourism development and through it for economic regeneration out of the present unsatisfactory state of affairs. It needs concerted action and urgently.

# 6

# Sustainable Tourism and Economic Development of the NE*

> Tourism has emerged as the biggest industry of the 21st Century, with international tourist arrivals expected to reach the staggering figure of 1.6 billion by 2020. In addition there is a huge number of domestic tourists which is about seven to eight times of the international tourists.

Tourism also has become a positive instrument of growth and development, of poverty alleviation and of redistribution of wealth. But such mass movement of people with the consequential requirement of the myriad services to be provided, naturally has impact on the nature and ecology. Therefore as the emphasis on tourism as an instrument for development grows, a corresponding concern for planning its development in a sustainable manner has become more audible.

The paper is divided into two major parts. In the first part the conceptual framework of tourism and sustainability are examined as they are relevant to the situation in the NE.

In the second part the economic scenario of the NE is briefly assessed and the role that tourism can play is examined. A framework for policy options is also attempted in this section.

---

* Paper presented in the Seminar on "Sustainable Development in the North East" Indian Council of Social Science Research. Shillong 21-23 October 2003.

## PART—I

### Why Tourism?—A Global View

Travel and tourism as an activity is as old as human civilization. But the importance of tourism as an economic activity came to focus only in the second part of the last century. In 1950 the total international tourist arrivals was 25 million and the total receipts from tourism was $ 2.1 billion. The number of arrivals multiplied two and half times during 1960 and 1970 and thereafter it has almost doubled every year. Between 1970 and 2000 the numbers increased tenfold—from 70 m to 700 m. Over the past 15 years the international tourism receipts have grown 1.5 per cent faster than the growth in world GDP.[1] The World Tourism Organisation (WTO) has forecast that by 2020 the arrivals figure would reach 1.6 billion and the receipts would be $2000 billion. In the recent past, tourism was affected by a variety of adverse factors like the terrorist attack of September 11 at New York and subsequently in Mombassa, Bali, Jakarta etc., the Afghan war and the Iraq war, the SARS, the slow economic recovery in the world's major tourism generating countries of USA, Japan, Germany. These factors caused the first dip in international tourism since WTO started keeping track fifty years ago. Yet such is the resilience of the industry and such is the experience of its recovery from similar crisis earlier like the Gulf War and Asian Economic Crisis that the WTO has not considered it necessary to revise its long term projection about its growth.

John Naisbitt in his book "Global Paradox"[2] had estimated in 1994 that tourism, with about 3.4 trillion in output was the largest industry of the world. By 1998, the World Tourism Organisation[3] reported that international tourism accounted for an estimated 8 per cent of the world's total export earnings and 37 per cent of exports in the services sector. International tourism receipts and passenger transport amounted to more than $504 billion, putting it ahead of all other categories of international trade as shown below—

| | *Category of trade* | *$ billion* |
|---|---|---|
| 1. | International tourism | 504 |
| 2. | Automotive products | 496 |
| 3. | Chemicals | 490 |
| 4. | Food | 458 |
| 5. | Petroleum and other fuels | 435 |
| 6. | Computers and office equipment | 394 |
| 7. | Textiles and clothing | 332 |
| 8. | Telecommunications equipment | 279 |
| 9. | Mining products | 163 |
| 10. | Iron and steel | 141 |

The contribution of tourism to socio-economic development of a country is now widely known and accepted. At the macro level, even a modest estimate by the WTO shows that tourism—

(a) Contributes 3-5 per cent of world GDP;

(b) Is one of the top five export items of 83 per cent countries of the world;

(c) Is the main source of foreign exchange earnings of at least 38 per cent countries of the world;

(d) Contributes about 11 per cent of the total direct employment of the world.

These are only some illustrative examples. The actual contribution of tourism is far more extensive. But tourism is a multi-dimensional activity and the measurement of its actual impact offers some practical difficulties. First, there is no clear definition of what constitutes tourism. The World Travel and Tourism Council (WTTC) has made a distinction between 'tourism industry' and 'tourism economy'. In common parlance, tourism is seen to be composed of a few activities like transport, accommodation, entertainment and other travel related services. These basic activities are called the 'Travel and Tourism Industry'. But the 'ripple effect' of tourism flows through a lot of other activities to the entire economy. WTTC has identified about 30 such activities to be at the core of travel and tourism business and calls it the 'Travel and Tourism Economy'. In making an assessment of the contribution of tourism to economic development of the NE, this distinction should be kept in mind.

Unfortunately, it is difficult to quantify the exact contribution of each of these sub-sectors. Because of difficulties in data collection and interpretation, tourism is often clubbed in the accounting process as 'invisible' and its contribution remains unnoticed. Many countries of the world have now adopted a new method of national accounting called the 'tourism satellite account' system with astounding results to show. Armed with such statistical evidence many countries have woken up to the potentials of tourism and have exploited their tourism resources as an important input in the economic development strategies. The WTTC, for example, believes that the contribution of travel and tourism to the world GDP is about 5.6 per cent and not 3-4 per cent as is commonly believed.

In spite of such inadequacies of accounting, the prominent role this sector can play in employment and income generation in the NE can be guessed from the experience at the national and global level. In 2001, tourism sector was estimated to have provided 17 million direct and 25 million indirect employment for the country. Rough official estimates of the multiplier effect of the tourism sector in employment creation put it at a high figure of 1:1.6. Considering the inadequacies of the accounting system as noted, these figures could be quite on the lower side. The Planning Commission's report on 'Targeting Ten Million Employment Opportunities' per year, projects a figure of 3.6 million jobs to be created in this sector alone.

An oft-quoted result of a sample survey conducted by the Ministry of Tourism illustrates the employment potentials of the tourism sector. It showed that for every million rupees invested at 1985-86 prices, the employment potential of different sectors are as follows:

| *Sector* | *Jobs* |
|---|---|
| Agriculture | 44.7 |
| Manufacturing | 12.6 |
| Mining and quarrying | 2.6 |
| Railways | 0.9 |
| Other transport | 13.8 |
| Tourism | 47.5 |
| Hotel and restaurants | 89.0 |

Another great advantage of tourism employment—an advantage which is of special relevance to the NE—is that it is not area specific. It could be promoted and developed anywhere. The spread effect of income and employment generation is therefore much larger than most traditional industries. Tourism being a service industry, is labour intensive and hard to automate or replace.

The NE of India is well-known for its rich heritage of culture and crafts. Tourism in general has very beneficial effect on promotion of art and local craft. A sample survey by the Ministry of Tourism has found some very interesting impact of tourism on the local artists and craftsmen. "The study indicates that about 96 per cent of total income of he artisan household in Kerala and about 90 per cent in Rajasthan comes from the tourism related artisan income. Exposure to tourism activities enhances the scope of employment generation, particularly in the lower income segment of the artisan household....As regards Folk Artists their average per capita income during the peak tourist season is nearly four times that in lean season in both the states."[4]

Tourism offers infinity of products and possibilities. It can be developed on the basis of intrinsic and natural advantages of a place or as can be seen from the experience of Disneyland, built purely out of human imagination. It can be built around natural beauty, history, art, culture, archaeology, sports, adventure, conventions and so forth. The NE has advantages in plenty in many of these spheres. The most important feature of tourism development is that it is an industry where the income is almost entirely a net accrual to the area.

**Tourism—Not an Unmixed Blessing**

However the experiences of many countries have shown that tourism is like a double-edged sword. Properly managed and implemented it can provide many benefits to the community. Unplanned and haphazard promotion of tourism, on the other hand can create many problems.

Such exponential growth of tourism as was experienced during the later part of the last century and is predicted for the coming years, will naturally have impact on the environment, ecology, culture, tradition and social behaviour. Broadly, unimaginative tourism planning can have adverse impact in three ways—

(a) on the eco-system—forests, wetlands, marine areas;
(b) on flora and fauna;
(c) on socio-cultural environment.

Environmental concerns are growing and therefore tourism practices, both good and bad, are now under close scrutiny of the world community. There are innumerable instances of tourism being the major source of income and livelihood for local communities. There are equally large number of instances of people being uprooted from natural habitat or losing traditional means of livelihood because of growth of tourism. The document, "Beyond the Green Horizon" brought out by the Worldwide Fund for Nature and 'Tourism Concern', for example, lists out an action agenda for sustainable tourism and also illustrates the pitfalls of unbridled growth of tourism by examples from around the world. It speaks of—

— Beach tourism development uprooting the fishing communities in Penang;

— Golf course constructions throwing out communities living for generations in Hana, Maui, Maunawili and Wainae in Hawaii;

— Coastal resort development in Thailand affecting the waters of Gulf of Thailand so that it no longer supports shellfish breeding in the area, throwing large number of traditional fishermen out of livelihood;

— Beach pollution and congestion in Philippines and most other popular beach resorts around the world because of tourism and unregulated constructions;

— Waste and litter left by mountaineers and trekkers polluting the snow areas of mountains in Nepal;

— Tourists destinations in Indonesia, in the French Pyrennes in the Mediterranean affected by waste, sewerage and pollution problems created by huge movement of tourists;

— The "loved to death" tendency of enthusiastic tourists visiting most national parks beyond the carrying capacity of the place, causing ecological damage.

Fortunately, such elaborate interest in sustainable tourism and documentation of the tourism practices both good and bad also points out to many cases where by sheer determination, imagination and people's participation adverse situations were transformed into positive examples of tourism. The BBC Report of 1992 ( the Natural World Portrait of the Planet, BBC II, 23rd February 1992) refers to 5,000 national parks and wildlife sanctuaries designed to be tourists attractions also serve as means of preservation and protection of flora and fauna. Naisbitt (1994) mentions some very delightful stories of positive tourism. In many countries sustainable eco-tourism is providing an alternative to unsustainable farming. In Rwanda, the Government was under strong pressure to cut the forests which were the natural habitat of the mountain gorillas, to make way for crops and cattle movement. Sensible tourism planning made it possible for the Government to save the forest habitat and to provide alternative and gainful source of income to the people by using the forest and the gorillas as parts of eco-tourism projects. In Kenya, forest protection was achieved under the community slogan "wildlife pays, so wildlife stays". In the Gulf of St. Lawrence in Canada, killing of baby seals in large number to make fashion garments made headlines in the 70s. Imaginative eco-tourism projects preserved the baby seals and provided the local population much higher income through tourism attractions based on these projects.

The lessons to be drawn from these examples are clear-that sustainability and mass tourism need not be conflicting objectives. Unimaginative tourism promotion can cause more harm than good but tourism carefully planned and properly implemented can benefit local culture, craft traditions, environment and eco-systems besides being source of income and employment. Mr. Frangialli, Secretary General of the WTO has pointed out[5] that the relationship between tourism and environment is symbiotic. Sustainable tourism is both necessary and possible because—

1. Travel and tourism promotes awareness about sustainable issues;
2. Well managed tourism is a good friend of the environment;
3. Tourism itself depends on a high quality of the environment and the eco-system.

**Sustainable Tourism—A Global Concern**

Though concern for the environment has been manifest throughout human civilization, visible and collective action at international level for sustainable development has been confined to the last part of the 20th Century. But the concern has been growing fast. Naisbitt (1994) mentions that more than 5 million Americans travelled every year only on nature related trips. Thirty million Americans belonged to various environmental organizations.

The World Development Report 2003 recounts the spectacular achievements of the world in the last fifty years but says:[6] "accompanying these achievements were some negative social and environmental patterns that must not be repeated in the next 50 years if development is to be sustained." Some of the concerns listed are—

— Poverty, declining but still a challenge. Almost 3 billion poor people earn less than $2 a day.

— Inequality widening. The average income of the richest 20 countries is 37 times that of the poorest 20.

— Fresh water, increasingly scarce. One-third of the world's people live in countries that are experiencing moderate to high water shortages. More than a billion people in low and middle income countries and 50 million people in high income countries lacked access to safe water for drinking, and domestic use in 1995.

— Soil degraded. Nearly 23 per cent of all cropland, pasture, forest and woodland worldwide have been degraded since 1950s.

— Forests being destroyed. Nearly one-fifth of all tropical forests have been cleared since 1960. According to 1997 World Resources Institute assessment, just one-fifth of the Earth's original forests remain in large, relatively natural ecosystems.

— Biodiversity disappearing. One-third of terrestrial biodiversity, accounting for 1.4 per cent of the Earth's surface, is in vulnerable 'hot spots' and is threatened with complete loss.

— Aquatic environment declining. About 58 per cent of the world's coral reefs and 34 per cent of all fish species are at risk from human activities.

Between 1987 when the landmark report of the Bruntland Commission—'Our Common Future'—was published and 2002, when the historic World Summit on sustainable development was held, there was a flurry of international activity on the subject as can be seen from a listing of some of the major events on the subject—

1. 1972—UN Conference on the Human environment, Stockholm;
2. 1980—Manila declaration on World Tourism;
3. 1987—Bruntland Commission report—Our Common Future;
4. 1992—The Rio Declaration and adoption of Agenda 21;
5. 1996—Adoption of Agenda 21 for the Travel and Tourism industry;
6. 1997—Male Declaration on Sustainable Tourism Development,

   Manila declaration on Social Impact of Tourism,

   Resolution of the 19th Special Session of the UN General

   Assembly requesting the Commission on Sustainable Development

   To develop an action oriented programme of work on Sustainable

   Tourism in co-ordination with WTO, UNEP and other UN bodies;
7. 1998—Resolution of the UN General Assembly proclaiming year 2002 as the International Year of Ecotourism;
8. 1999—WTO adopts Global Code of Ethics;
9. 2001—UN General Assembly adopts resolution on importance of responsible and sustainable tourism;
10. 2002—World Summit on Ecotourism;
11. 2002—World Summit on Sustainable Development.

There were numerous other sectoral events and initiatives on various components of sustainable development like development of coastal areas, development of small islands, biodiversity, culture, prevention of child labour, prevention of child sex and the like.

As can be seen, till 1997 the issue of 'sustainable tourism' was not independently and seriously discussed in the UN system. Even the much discussed Rio Declaration was heavily environment focused and did not mention tourism as such. The Agenda 21 which was the action programme of the Rio Declaration, did take tourism into consideration but not in an integrated manner. The UN General Assembly in its 19th Session, while reviewing the progress of implementation of Agenda 21, however acknowledged the importance of tourism. The Commission on Sustainable Development in its seventh session in 1999 organised a multi-stakeholders dialogue on sustainable tourism and accorded the status of an economic sector to tourism.

**Sustainable Tourism—The Concept**

Sustainable tourism is covered within the overall concept of sustainable development. The concept of sustainable development, though very widely used, is difficult to define. Any definition runs the risk of leaving out more than what it covers. However till today the definition adopted in the Bruntland Commission's report is accepted as the most comprehensive one. It defines sustainable development as "development that meets the needs of the present without compromising the ability of the future generations to meet their own needs." It elaborates sustainable development in essence as "a process of change in which the exploitation of resources, the direction of investments, the orientation of technological development and institutional changes are all in harmony and enhance both current and future potential to meet human needs and aspirations."

This definition has also been criticized as being not positive enough and as more emphasizing the negative aspects. Sustainable development, it is said, should go beyond the concern for the physical to the societal and cultural values.

The thrust of the Report, it is said did not adequately reflect the pressing concerns of poverty and economic sustainability. In fairness it has to be said that the report does for the first time focus on the essential needs of the world's poor to which priority attention should be paid though it does not define the concept of 'needs'. Subsequent discussions have drawn attention to the need to balance the interests of current and future generations and to the moral obligations of the present generation to ensure that the future generations enjoy at least as good a quality of life as the present. Such concerns for intergenerational equity are built around the concepts of economic, social and environmental sustainability.

Numerous interpretation and explanations of the term over the years have brought out some key elements of the concept. These may be summed up as—

1. Human poverty is at the core of the concern for sustainable development. The concept of 'needs' of the world's poor, therefore is an important element of the concept of sustainable development.
2. The concept has to be seen in a comprehensive manner, in the totality of the social, economic, environmental and cultural issues. The WTO[7] refers to the right balance between social, economic and environmental goals for achieving sustainable development. According to the results of the preparatory meetings of the World Summit on Sustainable Development, the overarching goal in the social field is poverty eradication; in economic field it is to change the unsustainable patterns of consumption and production and in the environmental field it is to achieve sustainable management of natural resources for development.
3. The main concern of sustainable development is the well-being of human beings and intergenerational equity. The assets compliment each other and therefore should be seen in totality.

4. The idea of balancing resources with present and future needs should not be seen as a static concern. Research, technological developments and human ingenuity continuously keep changing the parameters of resource availability.
5. Social, economic and environmental concerns need not be always in conflict. Such conflicts arise only in pursuit of individual or group gains without concern for the others. Positive state intervention in favour of the disadvantaged groups or individuals is needed for sustainable development.

The Agenda 21 drawn up at the Earth Summit is an exhaustive list of actions which are to be taken to give shape to the issues of sustainable development. The numerous suggestions are based on 27 principles of sustainable development programmes. The major principles relevant to the present study can be briefly stated as follows:[8]

1. Human beings are at the centre of concerns for sustainable development.
2. The right to development must be fulfilled, meeting the equitable needs of the present and the future generations.
3. The task of eradicating poverty is an indispensable requirement for sustainable development.
4. Global action and partnership is needed to conserve, protect and restore the eco-system.
5. States should reduce and eliminate unsustainable patterns of production and consumption.
6. States should promote endogenous capacity building for growth of new and innovative technologies.
7. States should encourage public awareness and participation.
8. States should take comprehensive measures for

environmental protection by enacting legislations, standards, etc.

9. Environmental impact assessment should be taken up as an instrument of action for all programmes likely to affect the ecology.
10. Indigenous people, communities and other local communities should play an effective and vital role and participate in the achievement of sustainable development.

It is quite clear that in this scenario tourism can play a very important role in sustainable development. This realization must have prompted the WTO to take a number of initiatives for promotion of the concept of sustainable tourism within the broad framework of sustainable development.

The WTO attempted a definition of sustainable tourism way back in 1988. As it was too soon after the report—Our Common Future—it did have the impact of the same. "Sustainable tourism development", it says[9] "meets the needs of the present tourists and host regions while protecting and enhancing opportunity for the future. It is envisaged as leading to management of all resources in such a way that economic, social and aesthetic needs can be fulfilled while maintaining cultural integrity, essential ecological processes, biological diversity and life support systems."

A sustainable tourism policy is evidently much wider than ecotourism or environmental preservation policy. Components of tourism like adventure tourism, rural tourism etc. would be part of such a policy and should not be confused with the bigger concept of sustainable tourism.

'Agenda 21 for the Travel and Tourism Industry'[10] has tried to draw up an action agenda for sustainable tourism in the pattern of Agenda 21 of the Earth summit. This agenda has identified the following nine priority areas:

1. Assess current regulatory, economic and voluntary

provisions for sustainable tourism and develop policies that facilitate sustainable tourism.

2. Assessing the economic, cultural, social and environmental implications of the organization's operations.
3. Develop and implement effective land use planning measures that maximize the potential environmental and economic benefits of travel and tourism.
4. Facilitate exchange of information, skills, and technology relating to sustainable tourism between developing and developed nations.
5. Ensuring participation of all sections of society, including women, indigenous people, the young and the old.
6. Design and develop new tourism products, in partnership with the private sector, that are sustainable economically, socially, culturally and environmentally.
7. Create awareness among all stakeholders and provide them with necessary skills to carry out tasks.
8. Establish realistic indicators of sustainable development applicable to local conditions and monitor progress.
9. Develop partnerships at all levels to facilitate responsible entrepreneurship.

The UN Economic and Social Council and the Commission on Sustainable Development in the 7th Session in 1999 discussed a large number of issues on tourism and sustainable development. From all such discussions it appears that any sustainable tourism development strategy or policy should take into consideration the following key elements:

1. Identifying the role of each of the stakeholders—the government, the industry and the people and creating partnership among them.
2. Participation of the community in the implementation

of sustainable development and their active role in it.

3. Creating awareness among all the players—among tourists, the host communities, the national and local tourism administration about their respective role.
4. Institutional mechanism for co-ordination among the key players.
5. Appropriate institutional and legal framework for regulation and control, which takes into account the special needs of specific areas.

Tourism, as we have mentioned, is a multi-dimensional activity. Within this broad framework of policy for sustainable tourism, there will naturally be wide variations in actual action agenda that different countries or regions adopt. The Agenda 21 on sustainable development has 170 action points. A programme of action for the NE must take into account the special needs of the area and the cultural, economic and social milieu of the region. Nevertheless examination of the successful practices of sustainable tourism and deliberations in various international fora[11] have identified some of the following as essential elements of any action programme—

1. Creating awareness about environmental ethics in tourism among communities and consumers.
2. Using resources sustainably—enforcing and adopting conservation and sustainable norms.
3. Reducing over consumption and waste.
4. Integrating tourism planning into the overall planning for sustainable development.
5. Involving local communities and supporting local economies; developing systems of consultations with the primary stakeholders.
6. Human resource development and training of personnel involved in sustainable tourism projects.
7. Ongoing enquiry into issues of sustainability and

research on environmental and ecological issues related to tourism.

8. Developing and using locally compatible tools for assessing and monitoring impact of tourism on environment, culture and heritage.

## PART—II

### Some Features of the Economic Scenario in the NE

The NE appears to be a compact geographical area but within this apparent compactness, there are wide variations in socio-economic situation. Any general statement about the economic situation in the region as a whole may therefore be inaccurate. A general assessment of the economic situation of any state must take into consideration issues like sectoral balances, income and employment generating measures, resource position, productivity and capital output ratios, nature of infrastructure development and investment opportunities and so on. In planning a development strategy, the socio-political issues of the area are also crucial parameters. However, in this section we will only briefly examine those features of the economic situation in the region which substantiate the thesis that tourism can and should play an important role in the economic planning of the region.[12]

#### *1. General Deceleration in the Economy*

The most striking feature of the economic development of the region has been a general downturn in economic performance compared to other states in the last few decades. It is reflected in the rate and pattern of growth of Net State Domestic Products (NSDP) and per capita income of the population. Dr. Gulshan Sachdeva[13] points out that "while the national economy is growing fast after initial contraction, the economies of the region are slowing down. In the decade of eighties growth rates in the North-Eastern Region were lower than the national growth rates. In the last few years the gap between national growth and regional growth rates has further widened."

However some of the states like Manipur, Tripura and Meghalaya showed higher growth rates during this period. Commenting on this Dr. Jayant Madhab[14] points out that this was mostly due to higher construction mainly roads activities financed by the Central Government in certain years. The most disturbing is the performance of the biggest economy in the region—Assam. At the time of Independence and the beginning of planned development in the country, Assam's per capita income was 4 per cent higher than the national at constant prices. By 1998-99 it was 41 per cent below the national average at current prices and 45 per cent below at 1980-81 prices. "What is even more alarming," states the Assam Development Report[15] "is that the gap is growing. Between 1980 and 1990, per capita income at 1980-81 prices grew by 20 per cent in Assam compared with 40 per cent for all-India. Between 1980 and 1998 per capita income in Assam grew by 10 per cent compared with 39 per cent for all India.... Assam's economy decelerated in the 1990s." It is very significant that this was the period of good growth for most states spurred by economic liberalization measures.

**2. *Higher Unemployment and Poverty***

Naturally, the stagnation in economic activities shows in fallout on human development indicators. For almost all the states the region the percentage of people below poverty line is substantially higher than the national average. The unemployment figures also show most states to be above the national average—the position of Assam again being alarmingly high. One further estimate quoted by Shri H.N. Das[16] shows that the percentage of unemployment among the youths of 15-29 age group has increased in Assam from 3.01 in 1983-84 to 19.25 in 1993-94 against the all-India figure of 6.46 per cent that year.

**3. *Distorted Sectoral Growth***

As is to be expected, neither industry nor agriculture has shown any significant growth during this period. In Assam, for example, in the 1990s the growth rate of agriculture slowed down to 1.6 per cent from the low figure of 2.1 of the earlier decade. Lower productivity of these sectors is compounded by disproportionate growth of the service sector. Dr. P.R. Bhattacharjee[17] shows (Annexure 5) that the tertiary sector has become unduly inflated owing to the tendency of the states to find employment in the public sector to accommodate the growing unemployed. This has led to lower productivity of investment leading further to lower income generation, resulting in lower expenditure in capital and development areas and therefore a continuing vicious cycle of underdevelopment. The resulting fiscal mismatch has found most of the states in serious financial distress and debt servicing has become one of the biggest components of the state expenditure. It increased from Rs. 733.34 crore in 1980 to Rs. 11,351.39 crore in 2001 in Assam and the fresh borrowing was almost eaten up by the interest payments. The Committee on Fiscal Reform set up by the Government of Assam pointed out that[18] "out of a total amount of Rs. 4,977.62 crore of un-earmarked fund in Assam's 9th Five Year Plan as much as Rs. 4,112.76 crore will be spent on salaries and establishment, constituting 82.62 per cent." The fact that 48.41 per cent of the earmarked fund also is spent on salaries and establishment should cause serious concern.

### 4. *'Unbalanced Economy'*

Prof. Sachdeva[19] has pointed out that the states of the region import food items worth about Rs. 2,000 to 2,500 crore annually. That a primarily agrarian and predominantly rural economy of the region should depend so heavily on the outside for primary food items reflects the weakness of the economic planning strategy. This weakness is further compounded by the fact that most of the export items of the region are primary resource based products like tea, petroleum products, plywood etc.

### 5. *Quality in HRD*

The region has fairly high levels of literacy rates. Some states like Mizoram are way above the national average. All other states except Arunachal Pradesh have literacy figures comparable to the national average or even higher. Yet, the number of trained teacher is only 45 per cent against the national average of 87 per cent. Prof. Sachdeva has quoted figures to show that in Assam and Nagaland only about 30 per cent of the higher secondary teachers are trained. Quality in human resource development should therefore be a major plank of economic development strategy.

**The Future Development Strategy**

In such a situation, the future strategy, naturally, will have to be multi-pronged but well coordinated, integrated and comprehensive. The strategy should focus on sectors that have high employment, income and employment generating capabilities and have strong backward and forward inter sectoral linkages. The Assam Development Report[20] has identified a few key elements of a future strategy for Assam. These are equally relevant for the rest of NE and are briefly mentioned below—

1. the development strategy should be based on the specific advantage of the place in natural resources;
2. The development process should be participatory—involving the community as well as the private sector;
3. Core growth sectors should be identified and thrust should be given to such sectors;
4. In the identification process, "priority should be given to those sectors, which have both comparative advantage and high linkages with other sectors";
5. Government has an important role to play and good governance should be part of the overall strategy;
6. Sound fiscal management is an integral part of the strategy.

Naturally the prescription is not exhaustive and every state has to tailor its requirement in the context of its own parameters. But because of its geographical isolation and distance from the primary markets and sources of raw materials, in the NE, investments based on locally available resources would be most cost effective. The economic situation also shows the precarious financial resource position of the states. Therefore, the investment portfolio should consist of projects which require the least government resources and which have the highest multiplier effect on income and employment. Investments which have higher dispersal effects on income and employment and which create more income locally, should get priority in the planning process.

**Tourism—The 'Hidden Jewel'**

The NE states need a sector of economic activity that can provide the much needed push to start the engine of growth from the present level of stagnation. Unfortunately the states have not given much attention to tourism so far, as an input in the development process either because the benefits of tourism are not so easily visible or because of their historical pre-occupation with the traditional sectors of growth. The ADR[21] is a refreshing departure from this approach and it clearly identifies tourism as one of the 8 thrust areas to play important roles in the new strategy.

We have mentioned earlier the crucial role tourism plays in the economies of many countries of the world. It will be instructive to recount the experience of Mexico as related by Mr. Antonio Savignac[22] former Minister of Mexico and Secretary general Emeritus of the WTO. In the 60s Mexico was experimenting with various models of growth to achieve a 6 per cent growth rate. Their exhaustive search and on going analysis kept coming back to the important role of tourism which the government had not noticed—'however, one of the curious activities that continually kept appearing was the case of tourism....a strange beast that seemed to grow like a weed with no fertilizer, irrigation care or attention.' He says, "we were amazed to find this hidden and, to us, unknown jewel....tourism an incredibly agile and flexible tool for social and economic development." The Mexican government concentrated on tourism as a key sector and the rest is history. Mexico developed as one of the top ten tourism countries in the world—earning for the country 8 billion dollars in 1997.

The NE can find similarities and lessons in the experience of Mexico. The region is in a similar situation of economic and financial doldrums that Mexico was in the 60s. The region has tourism potential and comparative advantage in its natural beauty, fauna, flora, ethnicity, history, archaeology and colourful mosaic of culture. These are the ingredients that can create the most important product quality that the modern tourists are looking for—'unique experience.'

**Tourism Scenario in the NE**

Unfortunately, the present picture of achievement does not reflect the potential of tourism in the NE. India itself is far away from realizing its true tourism potential. But the figures for the NE compared to the national figures are insignificant. The arrival figures of tourists both domestic and international, make this abundantly clear.[23]

| | *1999* | *2000* | *2001* | *2005* |
|---|---|---|---|---|
| Arunachal Pradesh | 1008/48 | 9932/2044 | 6349/ 323 | 305/289 |
| Assam | 14336/604 | 891433/5954 | 1010651/6171 | 2467652/10782 |
| Manipur | 97523/277 | 105167/429 | 76527/183 | 94299/316 |
| Meghalaya | 159730/1971 | 169929/2327 | 178697/2390 | 375901/5099 |
| Mizoram | 27139/216 | 28221/235 | 28771/152 | 44715/273 |
| Nagaland | 21041/119 | 13272/451 | 9946/920 | 17470/883 |
| Sikkim | 138785/8554 | 143105/10409 | 203306/31028 | 151744/16523 |
| Tripura | 246507/335 | 231902/0 | 254912/0 | 216330/2677 |
| *All India* | *190671014/5832105* | *22106941/5893542* | *234200935/5427366* | *390466880/9939782* |

The total number of approved hotels and the room capacity also shows the poor state of infrastructure.

*(2005)*

| | *No. of approved hotels* | *No. of rooms* |
|---|---|---|
| Arunachal Pradesh | | |
| Assam | 4 | 272 |
| Manipur | — | — |
| Meghalaya | 1 | 50 |
| Mizoram | 1 | 28 |
| Nagaland | | |
| Tripura | | |
| Sikkim | 1 | 28 |

It is quite possible that the figures suffer from deficiencies in statistical compilation. So far hotels are concerned, it is quite likely that most of the accommodation is in the unorganized sector and do not come under the purview of the government. In either situation one cannot escape the conclusion that the state of affairs is far from satisfactory.

**How to Go Forward?—Some Elements of a Future Strategy**

Based on the foregoing analysis some agenda for action for promotion of sustainable tourism in the NE can be suggested.

The core elements of strategy for action have been aptly summed up in the following diagram by the Agenda 21 for Travel and Tourism[24]—

**Perception:** It is essential to start with a correct perception about the role of tourism in the economic development of the region. Unfortunately, in spite of its comparative advantage in this area, tourism is not perceived as an important economic activity. The first task of the governments should be to create awareness about the place of tourism in general and of sustainable tourism in particular.

tourism's importance and provide it due priority in the planning process.

**The Starting Point-domestic Tourism:** Domestic tourism plays a very key role in Indian tourism. Against the average ratio of about 7 domestic tourists per one foreign tourist in the total picture internationally, in India the ratio is about 1:80. In absolute terms the figure of total domestic tourists is about 235 million against 2.5 million foreign tourists. The NE has a very insignificant share of this huge number of tourists who contribute to employment and income generation in other states. Movement of domestic tourists will slowly improve the image of the place and the demand created will lead to development of essential infrastructure. This process will then facilitate movement of foreign tourists who normally expect a higher standard of infrastructure.

**A Broad NE Perspective in Planning:** Because of its geographical position tourism planning of the NE states, whether aimed at the domestic or the foreign tourists, would be most attractive and cost effective if based on an integrated NE perspective. Globally also, regional cooperation in tourism has been the new strategy and many institutional arrangements for such regional tourism have developed. The attractions of the different states, rather than competing, should supplement each other and enhance the total attraction of the region. Unfortunately this vital necessity of projecting the totality of NE tourism suffers from two fundamental inadequacies—

1. Poor internal communication between the states. The road communication is arduous and time consuming. Air communication of late has improved, but is not yet tuned to tourism requirements. Coordinated planning of tourism for the NE is possible only when the internal communication by air becomes efficient and reliable.
2. Lack of organizational set up. There is no organizational set up that can harmonise action for projecting NE tourism as a whole. Prospective tourists

who want to visit and sympathetic entrepreneurs who want to market the NE find it exasperating to draw up an integrated schedule for the whole region. There is too much of dependence on the government and too little incentives for the private sector to enable them to play an effective role. If tourism in the NE has to grow, a common platform of all the states, involving the government and the non-governmental agencies should be immediately set up.

**A Definite Policy:** The first requirement is to move away from ad hoc measures in tourism to a definite plan of action and direction of future movement. Every state must bring out a pragmatic tourism policy not couched in general terms but clearly charting a plan of action. It should indicate the government's commitment to sustainable tourism, the place assigned to tourism in the broad development planning, the role of government and of the other key players. It should identify the organizational pattern to implement the policy and a system of monitoring and accountability.

**An integrated Policy:** Tourism policy would remain the wish list of the tourism department alone unless it reflects total government commitment. Tourism being a multi-dimensional activity, depends on the involvement of the other departments for its success. Other departments like roads, culture, forest and so on can play a very important role in the development of the total tourism product. For achieving maximum coordination, institutional arrangements should be put in place—the ideal arrangement being an effective policy planning and implementation Board under the chairmanship of the Chief Minister.

**Organisational Structure to Implement the Policy:** Most well intentioned policies fail due to weakness in implementation. Weaknesses in implementation arise when the organization in place is insufficient to achieve the desired objectives. The NE needs a tourism organization which is professionally managed, capable of taking quick decisions and is accountable. It is suggested that an Autonomous Tourism Development Board with private sector participation should be considered by each state. It should have a high profile, ideally being chaired by the Chief Minister and including representatives of key departments of the government, so that interdepartmental coordination can be achieved quickly.

**How to meet the resource gap?** The state of infrastructure development in the NE would require a lot of attention if tourism has to grow at a fast rate and has to become competitive. In the context of very precarious financial position of most of the states, lack of resources may sap any new initiative on the tourism sector. For example, the Assam Development Report has assessed that to achieve a growth rate of 6 per cent in the economy the quantum of investment required in the Trade, Hotels and Restaurants sector would be around Rs. 7,984 crore for the next five years. As such levels of investment are not available, the normal reaction would be to forget about the idea. However, pragmatic thinking may find possible solutions to the problems of resources. In this connection, a comprehensive approach involving the following guidelines are suggested:

1. *A benchmark survey of tourism assets:* The general approach to tourism planning has been ad hoc because there is no comprehensive assessment of the resources and the potential. Tourism planning should start with a benchmark survey in each district of the tourism potential of the area. The survey should identify and classify the tourism products according to their importance into three categories—local, regional and national and international.
2. *Prioritise—a selective approach:* Because of the compulsions of the democratic governance system, there is a tendency to take up too many schemes in a routine unimaginative manner to satisfy local aspirations. As a result the investments fail to have any visible effect and impact. Instead, the source of

funding of tourism projects and the quantum should depend on the relative importance from the point of view of the tourists. The projects which satisfy primarily local demand should be included in the District Development Plans. The schemes of regional importance should be included in the state plan schemes and those which are of national and international importance should be taken up with the assistance of the national government and international agencies. A **Master Plan** for these schemes should be prepared and allocation of fund should be based on the integrated plan of development.

Naturally, a comprehensive strategy would also require that the governments allot more fund than they are doing at present for tourism development. A planned and integrated approach would mean that with the available resources more effective investments can be made.

3. *Tourism focus in other department's schemes:* A tourism product cannot be developed by the tourism department alone. There should be general government policy that in respect of the identified areas and schemes, the other departments like roads, forest and culture should give relative priority to tourism components in their schemes.
4. *Build partnership with the private sector:* Tourism is primarily a private sector driven industry. A dynamic private sector can reduce the pressure on the government by taking on a lot of activities for tourism development. The concept of partnership is much wider than the commonly used expression of private participation. It implies a system of formalized cooperation between the government and private sectors where the partners share responsibilities, resources, risks and rewards. Unfortunately private initiatives in the tourism sector in the NE have been

negligible. The nature of partnership varies from country-to-country. The nature of partnership also is not limited to any particular areas and would depend on the local requirements and initiatives of the planners. In the NE some of the areas where such partnership can be very meaningful are—

(a) Financing of new infrastructure projects;

(b) Evolving a modern, focused, comprehensive and intensive marketing collaboration;

(c) Collaborating in human resource development;

(d) Sharing development, beautification and maintenance of various tourism products;

(e) Participating in the preservation of the heritage;

(f) Providing leadership in creating awareness about sustainable norms by adopting good practices in the industry.

**Prepare an Ecology Map:** To ensure that mismanaged tourism does not damage eco-system and environment, government has to play a resolute and definite role. Synergy can be achieved only when the approach is systematic and planned. For this purpose—(a) Each State should prepare an ecology map of the possible tourism destinations and zones. The zones should be graded according to the fragility of the eco-system. (b) The nature of tourism planning will depend on the degree of fragility of the eco-system. Areas which are very fragile may even be closed to mass tourism and developed only for special interest group tourism like adventure tourism. (c) In other words, tourism development in these identified areas should depend on two factors—carrying capacity studies and environmental impact assessment studies. Any product development in these areas should be preceded by a project appraisal which includes these studies.

**Design Architectural Norms:** Architecture is part of the cultural heritage of a place. Unimaginative construction may not only spoil the tradition of the place but can also adversely affect the ecology of the place. Every architecture should suit the local conditions and should blend with the environment around. Unaesthetic construction practices have been the bane of most hilly areas which have beautiful designs coming down the centuries. It would be useful for the NE to develop an architectural code that embodies the heritage of the place, takes into account the ecological and aesthetic requirements and blends tradition with modern needs, based on local skills and are functionally efficient. Government should make such a code obligatory for any new construction.

**Legal and Institutional Framework for Sustainable tourism:** Even though there are plenty of regulations for the preservation and control of the environment both at the state level and at the Centre, many of them have become quite obsolete and irrelevant. Many of them do not address the emerging problems of the present day nor do they offer modern solutions. In most case implementation is slack and often they are implemented in isolation, often too rigidly by the controlling department without proper appreciation of the spin off problems created for other sectors. Government should therefore put in place a set of pragmatic legislations which are in tune with the general government policy, and which can be easily implemented. In particular the states and the center should:

(a) Make an inventory of all the existing legislations on environmental issues;

(b) Weed out the obsolete ones;

(c) Frame new legislations which cover areas hitherto uncovered and reflect regional variations and avoid stereotype rigidity in implementation;

(d) Ensure strict implementation;

(e) For most effective implementation, public support should be enlisted by setting up monitoring mechanism involving the public.

Participatory implementation is the only solution to the

problem of environmental protection and departmental coordination is the basic requirement for its success. The WTO has drawn up extensive action agenda for sustainable tourism in the form of Code of Ethics. It will be useful for the governments of the NE to adopt the basic issues of the Code and give it wide publicity.

**Creating Institutions for People's Participation:** "A mistake made by the community is thousand times better than a solution imposed by an expert"(Mexican proverb). We have seen that intergenerational well-being of the people is a fundamental objective of sustainable development. The local community should therefore be actively involved in planning tourism and also in sharing the benefits of tourism. Agenda 21 had recommended formation of local Agenda 21 committees and in many parts of the world such local committees have been formed and local agenda have been drawn up. It would be ideal if such local agenda can be drawn up in the NE for tourism.

Even if such elaborate arrangements, though desirable, cannot be immediately put in place, government should ensure people's participation by forming local advisory committees for tourism wherever prominent tourism attractions exist and also having such committees at the state level. Such arrangements will give a sense of belonging to the people and will improve the efficiency of operations of projects and tourism products.

**Human Resource Development:** Tourism is a service industry and therefore the quality of the service makes a substantial difference in the demand for the tourism product. Human resource development should therefore be an important part of the future strategy for tourism development in the region. It will also be in tune with the objective of employment generation through tourism.

Sustainable tourism in particular depends on awareness and understanding, both of the tourist as well as the host community. The tourist has to be educated on the cultural ethos and the ecological concerns of the community. The human resource development should encompass training of all people who come to contact with the tourist at the cutting edge level like the tour operators, the travel agents, the tour guides, the taxi drivers—all ranges of tourism managers who can educate the tourist.

It is difficult to identify all the diverse areas which tourism covers on which action is to be taken. More than stating the action points the agenda should focus more on implementation. A strong commitment to sustainable tourism, a determined plan of action and a devotion to proper implementation will be the crucial factors if NE decides to take advantage of its god gifted assets for betterment of the lot of the people.

## REFERENCES

1. Bezbaruah, M.P., *Frontiers of New Tourism*. Gyan Publishing House. New Delhi, 2002, p. 19.
2. Naisbitt, John. William Morrow and Company. New York, 1994, p. 104.
3. WTO. *The Economic Impact of Tourism*. Undated brochure.
4. Ministry of Tourism, Government of India. *Tourist Statistics*, 2001, p. 137.
5. Frangialli, Francesco. *Observations on International Tourism*. WTO, Madrid. 1999.
6. The World Bank. World Development Report 2003. *Sustainable Development in a Dynamic World*. Oxford University Press. New York, 2003, pp. 2-3.
7. WTO, 2002, WTO Contribution to the World Summit on Sustainable Development, Johannesberg, 2002. WTO. Madrid.
8. United Nations. 1992. Agenda 21: Programme of Action for Sustainable Development. United Nations. New York, pp. 9-11.
9. WTO. Undated. *Agenda 21 for the Travel and Tourism Industry: Towards Sustainable Development*, p. 30.
10. WTO, *op. cit.*, pp. 40-52.
11. In particular, reference may be made to the following—"Beyond the Green Horizon" World Wide Fund for Nature; the Bali Declaration (1996) and the Male Declaration (1997) of the WTO; the Agenda 21 for the Travel and Tourism Industry (WTO); the Earth Summit and Rio Declaration (1992); the World Conference on Sustainable Tourism and Heritage Management (1996).
12. This section draws heavily from "Tourism and Economic Development of

the NE States"—a unpublished paper by M.P. Bezbaruah presented in the seminar on 'NE in the Age of Globalisation' organized by Institute of Applied Manpower Research, New Delhi, 4-5 March 2003.

13. Sachdeva, Dr. Gulshan. "North –Eastern Economy: Past Policies, Present Realities and Future Possibilities" unpublished paper presented in the Seminar on 'North-East: Challenges and Response' at Nehru Memorial Museum, New Delhi, 19-21 December 2002.
14. Madhab, Dr. Jayant. "Commentary on the Fiscal Situation of the North-Eastern States". *Dialogue.* Vol. 4. No 1. 2002, p. 46.
15. Planning Commission. Government of India. Assam Development Report, 2002, p. 1.
16. Das, H.N. "The Present Financial Crisis in Assam". *Dialogue.* Vol. 4. No 1, 2002, p. 95.
17. Bhattacharjee, Dr. P.R. "The Problem of Ensuring Financial Efficiency in the North-Eastern States". *Dialogue.* Vol. 4, No. 1, 2002. p. 66.
18. Das, H.N., *op. cit.,* p. 88.
19. Sachdeva, Dr. Gulshan, *op. cit.*
20. Planning Commission, *op. cit.,* 2002, pp. iii-v.
21. *Ibid.,* p. iv.
22. Savignac, Antonio,1998. "The Importance of Tourism as an Instrument for Social and Economic Development." Foundation Day Lecture, Ministry of Tourism, New Delhi. 25 January1998. Quoted in 'Indian Tourism Beyond the Millennium' by M.P. Bezbaruah, Gyan Publishing House, New Delhi, 2000, pp. 124-126.
23. Ministry of Tourism, *op. cit.,* 2001, p. 56.
24 WTO. Undated. Agenda 21 for the Travel and Tourism Industry. *op. cit.,* p. 39.

# 7

# Tourism and Economic Development of Assam

> "Everything has been thought of before, but the problem is to think of it again" —Goethe

This paper does not intend to go into detailed analysis of the economic realities of Assam or of the nuances of tourism development. Both would be fascinating studies, but for the sake of brevity, the paper is confined to an analysis of the broad parameters only.

In this analysis tourism is considered as an 'input' in the total development process. Many of us tend to see in our own small world of expertise the whole world encompassed and do not look beyond. Sometimes we talk of tourism as the only solution. Nothing could be more damaging to constructive thinking on development or to promotion of tourism itself. Tourism has to be seen as one of the inputs, may be a key one depending on the situation of any particular place that we discuss. Its success will depend on how we coordinate and integrate with the other important inputs.

Before prescribe tourism is prescribed as a possible solution for Assam's economic ills, it is necessary to know the nature of ailment itself. Fortunately, the main features of the present economic situation of the state and for that matter of the NE in general have been fairly well studied and documented. We can recapitulate the same.

* First Napolean Hazarika memorial lecture of the North Eastern Economic Association at Guwahati, Assam on December 30, 2002.

First is the disturbing and what the recent Assam Development Report (ADR) calls the most striking fact of Assam's economic development that it is continuously falling behind the national economy. At the beginning of the planning process Assam's per capita income was 4 per cent higher than the national average. By 1998, it was 41 per cent below the national average. As pointed out by Dr. Atul Sarma, Assam, which was the fifth largest in per capita, is now the lowest after Bihar. Between 1980 and 1998 per capita income in Assam grew by 10 per cent compared to 39 per cent for national.

This dismal picture is the result of two primary factors—the economy was growing at a slower rate and a population growing at a faster rate than the national average shared the smaller pie. Till 1979, though the per capita income was falling because of higher population growth, the economy's growth was more or less comparable to the national average. And when in the 1990s with economic reforms and all that the Indian economy was growing at a rate of 6 per cent Assam's State GDP growth rate was only 3.3 per cent. In fact during the 1990s the economy decelerated. According to the draft Tenth Plan document the growth rate of Assam during the 8th and 9th plan was a meager 2.8 and 2.1 only.

Naturally this is a reflection of poor performance by the sectors. The most telling impact has been of slower growth rate in the agriculture sector—declining to 1.6 per cent per year in the 1990s against already low figure of 2.1 per cent. With 89 per cent of the population living in the rural areas, the impact of declining agricultural productivity is bound to be far reaching. It shows in higher incidence of people below poverty line and in higher unemployment among the youth. The ADR reports that Assam is the only state that showed increasing rural poverty over a long period from 1957 to 1994. The ratio of people below poverty line of 36 per cent is much higher than the national average of 26 per cent. Similarly, an estimate has shown that the percentage of unemployment among the youths of 15-29 age group has increased in Assam from 3.01 in 1983-84 to 19.25 in 1993-94 against an all India average of 6.46.

Of the other two sectors, growth has been more or less stagnant. The manufacturing sector is reported to have declined from 6.5 per cent in 1990 to 5.4 per cent in 1997. Tertiary sector has shown some growth but it is, as pointed out, a distorted growth. While transport, storage and communication rose only marginally public administration rose substantially to 7 per cent by 1997-98.

It is no wonder that dismal position of the public finances stand out as the most difficult problem of economic management of the state. The gross fiscal deficit for the year 2001-02 has been estimated at Rs. 2500 crore. The enormous importance of sound public finance management for the future planning of Assam is undeniable, but for our limited interest of today, leaving aside the broader issues, I would like to point out a few very obvious but disturbing trends, which need to be corrected.

First, there is a big mismatch between growth of total receipts and total expenditure. While for the last five years the expenditure is rising at a rate of 5.4 the expenditure is growing at a rate of 12.9.

Deficit financing in itself may not be such a serious concern. Many countries, including ours resorted to deficit financing as a part of planned strategy for development. But in this case it is not part of a deliberate policy and its wayward nature creates more problems every passing day. The expenditure is largely not productive and is neither creating any productive assets nor leading to multiplier effects on income. Let me quote the words of a former Chief Secretary and Chairman of the Committee on Fiscal Reform (CoFR) "...the proportion of capital expenditure has come down to less than 12 per cent while that of revenue expenditure has increased to more than 88 per cent. This is scandalous to put it mildly."

One is even more alarmed to see the composition of the expenditure. It reflects a vicious cycle of poverty and debt trap. Assam spent 78 per cent of total expenditure in 2000-01 in salary, pension, interest payments and repayment of loan. According to the COFR "out of a total amount of Rs. 4,977.62 crore of unearmarked funds in Assam's Ninth Five Year Plan, as much as Rs. 4,112.76 crore will be spent on salaries and establishments, constituting 82.62 per cent. Out of a total allocation (including both earmarked and non-earmarked fund) of Rs. 8,496.06 crore the expenditure on salary and establishment will also be high at 48.41 per cent."

In such a dismal situation, one can look for many ways to get out of the mess. Obviously higher revenue generating efforts, greater dedication to reducing expenditure, etc., would form part of the strategy. It will be natural also to look at the market forces to provide more fillip to exports from the region to bring in more income. Unfortunately, here we find only a reverse flow. Dr. Gulshan Sachdeva has mentioned that the NE imports food items worth about Rs. 2000-2500 crore annually from other parts of the country. There is no firm figures of Assam's imports, but various estimates had put it between Rs. 1000-1500 crore for food items alone.

The instruments of "commanding heights" the Public Sector Undertakings could be expected to provide the much needed sectoral push if not contributing financially to the state exchequer. On both counts the position is pathetic. The total accumulated loss of the PSUs stood at a staggering figure of Rs. 4060 crore. Of the 49 PSUs 30 had fully eroded their net worth.

Naturally two questions should be asked—what caused this and how to get out of it? The ADR has found some clearly marked periods and consider 1980 to be the watershed after which the downward slide began. As the period also coincided with the emergence of agitation and conflict as the weapon for redressal of socio-economic grievances, it is tempting to establish correlation ship between the two.

However any attempt to establish linear relationship between the two would be too simplistic an approach. Nevertheless this issue needs to gone into very carefully and deeply, at least to caution the future generations about the pitfalls on our way.

Fiscal situation is one area of major concern, but let us not confuse it with the bigger and wider malaise of economic development—involving issues of resource management, productivity, and a host of other economic issues. Fiscal problem is primarily a management issue and not the cause of economic backwardness or lack of economic activity. In fact in most cases it is the effect of backwardness. Many committees have been formed on the subject and many valuable suggestions have been offered. Purposeful, firm action will have to be taken on them urgently before the situation gets totally out of hand.

Almost everyone blames the recommendations of the 5th Pay Commission for the adverse impact on the finances of the states. In rational economic terms it can have two interpretations. In a market economy, every functionary has a service to offer for which payments are made. If the additional payments flowing from the Commission's recommendations are to cause such imbalance then either the additional services performed falls far short of the productive level or the number of people required to provide the present level of services should be much smaller. Either the same level of bureaucracy should handle a much larger area of activity in the coming years without any addition to the workforce or a smaller number should handle the present level of activities. In either scenario, one thing is certain; public administration cannot be looked upon as the primary provider of employment in the future. We have to look at other options and tourism is one of them.

Devolution of central resources and injustice in doing so is another complaint often repeated. In this connection, the following statement from the Chairman of the Committee on

Financial Reforms, Shri Haren Das—is interesting—"the Eleventh Finance Commission, for example, drastically cut down the resource gap of Rs. 36,189.84 crore as assessed by the Government of Assam to a paltry sum of Rs. 110.68 crore only. This happened due to a mistake in calculation by the Commission's office."

This unfairness, it would seem, is not a post independence phenomenon but the legacy goes back to 1919. In an interesting article in a recent seminar, Prof. Imdad Hussain has recounted the history of Assam's woes and laments. Sir Md Sadullah had lamented before the Constituent Assembly in August 1949 that the Montague-Chelmsford Reforms as the period when "the greatest injustice was done to a poor province of Assam." Montague-Chelmsford Report it may be recalled was the first financial reform proposing complete separation of central and provincial revenues. The Government of India Act 1919 gave expression to this reform and the Financial Relations Committee called the Meston Report worked out the distribution of revenues and contributions by the states to wipe out the deficits of the center. In this process Assam had to contribute Rs. 15 lakh, Bihar and Orissa nil, on a principle based on 'capacity to pay' and on an assumption of a surplus budget of Assam. Even at that time Assam had cried foul and alleged that the Meston Committee had not taken into account Assam's contributions in excise on petrol and kerosene etc. It was all ignored and the Reforms started the procession of deficit budgets for the state with only a few exceptional years. The government sought to meet the situation by additional taxation but the Legislative Council refused to pass additional levies. Nilomoni Phukan's eloquent protests in the first session of the Council in 1921 were widely acclaimed.

Assam continued the plea for special treatment and lament for injustice—in words and arguments similar to our memorandum of today—before the Simon Commission. But all this was of no avail—Assam got no relief and the financial settlement under the Government of India Act 1935 was dubbed as discriminatory by all and sundry in Assam. Bishnuram

Medhi, presenting the last budget before independence told the Legislative Assembly of "the financial injustice" meted out to the state. Bordoloi and Sadullah jointly took up Assam's case in the Constituent Assembly, but the historians record that the Constituent Assembly only perpetuated the inequities of the colonial legacy.

Implicit in this long story of neglect and discrimination, both colonial and post independence, is an underlying message signaled by Sir Sadullah as early as in 1933-34 that "Assam being the smallest province in India, has no voice in the Councils of the higher authorities." In a federal democracy, the regions' benefits will be directly proportionate to the political power and presence in the center. In democratic governance based on alliances, political positioning for economic gains becomes even more important. There is no doubt that our presence in the power base has been weak and our political representation and voice in the center even weaker.

What is the future scenario? The ADR analysis of the possible scenario only shows how daunting the task is. The report shows that it will be difficult for Assam to catch up with the national average even in 50 years time. But it is more important to see that the economic growth does not decelerate any further.

The ADR has a 25-year projection for the Assam economy to catch up with the national average. Assuming the national economy grows at 4 per cent, a 6 per cent growth rate for the first 10 years and 7 per cent thereafter can bring Assam at par with the country in 25 years. If the national economy grows at 6 per cent constant rate, Assam's growth rate will have to be 6 per cent for the first 5 years 8 per cent for the next five and 9 per cent thereafter. If the national economy grows at 8 per cent as targeted for the 10th Plan, and if that target remains the same if not higher for the next plans, Assam's performance will have to be much higher in the short run or the period will have to be extended beyond 25 years. With a present growth rate of 2 per cent only, even with a superlative effort it may not be possible for Assam to suddenly step up the tempo and therefore it seems inevitable that Assam should reconcile to a position of underdevelopment compared to the national economy for a long time to come.

The only way out is to be seized of the urgency of the matter and to go all out to step up the economic activities. But even here there are problems and uncertainties galore. First, the present investment pattern does not instill any hope. From 1980 to 1998, the gross rate of capital formation at 17.2 per cent of GSDP is 7.5 per cent behind national. Unless this difference is narrowed, catching up will remain a difficult proposition. Even to achieve 6 per cent growth rate, the investment required is much higher than what is currently available. In 2002-03, the plan allocation for the state is only about 40 per cent of the estimated investment required to launch Assam on the growth path.

How to expand the investment base? Where will the resources come from? Two of the seven states of the NE, Dr. Jayant Madhab has pointed out, are on the verge of bankruptcy. Rural development schemes of government of India, which require 25 per cent state contribution, cannot be availed of because the states do not have the resources for such contribution. As a result will the vicious cycle of poverty continue?

To break the cycle, some of the areas we have to give attention are—

1. Get more resources within the public sector from Centre. This is possible from three sources—
   (a) Devolution through the Finance Commission grants, which we have already talked about.
   (b) State Plan outlays—Assam has got an allocation of Rs. 8,315 crore for the 10th Plan, which is a substantial increase. In fact, the central assistance is even higher—Rs. 9,527 crore, but the final

figures come down because the state's own resources is a minus figure. It is pertinent to mention that often the public knowledge about the plan size can be quite misleading. The Plan consists of primarily the following—

States' Own Resources, (SOR) which includes Balances from

Current Revenues, Internal Resource Mobilization,

Resources of Public Sector Undertakings, Extra Budgetary

Resources and Borrowings;

—Central Financial Assistance (CFA).

Quite often the very big size of plan is announced on the assumption of higher and promised resource generation by the state, which, if they do not materialize, deflates the plan size automatically. The crucial component for the state is the CFA, which normally does not increase by more than 20 per cent. The NE has already got substantial benefit in the composition of the assistance itself—90 per cent of it being grant. It is not likely that the benefits can be extended very much to make any meaningful dent in the investment position.

(c) However, the third category—Central Sector Plan Schemes—is an area, which should be looked at more closely. The Central share of the public sector investment in the Plan is much larger than all the states taken together and it is growing as shown below—

**Plan Allocations**

| | *9th Plan* | *Percentage* | *10th Plan* | *Percentage* |
|---|---|---|---|---|
| Centre | 4,06,687 | 57.6 | 9,21,291 | 57.8 |
| State | 2,99,131 | 42.3 | 6,71,009 | 42.14 |

**State Plans**

| | *9th Plan* | *10th Plan* |
|---|---|---|
| Central Assistance | 1,38,394 | 3,00,265 |
| State's Own resources | 1,60,737 | 3,70,744 |

The Central portion was 46.2 per cent of the total state Plan in the 9th Plan and 44.7 per cent in the 10th. Thus it is clear that the central share of the state plan is not increasing. At the same time the central Plan size is growing bigger. It is important therefore to look at the greater share of the Central schemes. So far perhaps the NE has not been able to take full advantage of the schemes because of a variety of reasons like-lack of information about the schemes, lack of matching grants, absence of expertise in project preparation, failure to implement schemes timely and inability to get fresh schemes for failure to submit utilization reports.

2. Proper utilization of funds available is therefore of crucial importance for that elusive economic push. Utilisation is not merely spending—it must lead to additional income generation and higher productivity. The importance of productivity is often not appreciated.

3. But the most important need is of stronger public-private partnership. It is necessary to get out of a general mindset in this region against private profit and against government incentives for the private sector. Private sector must be provided an atmosphere where initiative can grow. If not incentives, at least the roadblocks created by large number of licenses should be rationalized to enable private entrepreneurship to flourish. The private sector should be neutralised at least against the disadvantages of distance from the market—both of raw materials and end products—and for lack of infrastructure

comparable to those available to competing regions. At the same time a pragmatic industrial policy should ensure that the outgo on the incentives given are more than matched by higher returns from the sector.

4. It is obvious that at this time higher mobilization of resources is very important. This can be done by plugging the loopholes in the present system, making revenue-collecting machinery more efficient and also by looking at new sources of revenue, which do not adversely affect the basic objectives of development.
5. However, it is most important to create an economic momentum by activating at least some sectors with good forward and backward linkages, so that the economy can get, so to say, a kick-start. It is refreshing to find that the ADR talks of 'Comparative advantage' as a criterion for economic policy choice and finds tourism to be one of the key sectors, which justifies attention for a definite policy thrust.

Why tourism? It would be most appropriate to quote the experience of Mexico as narrated by Antonis Savignac former minister.

**"The Story Begins in the Mid-60s...**

The aim of the government was to achieve a 6 per cent average annual real rate of growth of the Gross Domestic Product (GDP), while maintaining a low level of inflation. The reason—to absorb an increase of population then about 3.5 per cent annually, and to provide 2.5 per cent for growth and social improvement.

The problem. 6 per cent growth meant an increase in production; increase in production meant increase in imports...increase in imports meant obtaining more foreign currency,...to pay for increased imports...

The search: an exhaustive on going analysis was made of all types of goods and services that could be exported: agriculture, fisheries, mining, manufactured and semi-manufactured goods, etc. All types of assumptions, combinations and projections were run through...

However, one of the curious activities that continually kept appearing was the case of tourism. Tourism to Mexico had been growing consistently and successfully in various destinations without any planning, fiscal incentives or credit facilities and despite whole series of red tape and lack of facilitation.

A strange beast that seemed to grow like a weed, with no fertilizer, irrigation, care or attention.

Knowing nothing about this activity we promptly set out to analyze it...

Our conclusions were surprising at least to us, who were novices in this field.

1. It could be developed and promoted almost anywhere.
2. It grew with little if any, government help, programmes or policies.
3. It offered infinity of products and possibilities such as business, conventions, cruise, nature (parks, lakes, mountains) archaeology, cities, sports, adventure, sun and beaches, culture, folklore, music, astronomy and so forth.
4. It was relatively free of restrictions, unlike other exports of goods and commodities, which were subject to quotas, taxes, import permits and many others.
5. Generally it did not consume non-renewable resources, nor did it involve dangerous processes.
6. It was labour intensive and, being a personal service, hard to automate or replace.
7. The technology for its development was well known and easily available,....
8. Training of personnel was generally easy, available and quick...

9. Foreign tourism was capable of providing an ever-increasing flow of foreign currency.
10. The foreign import component of the industry was exceptionally low ...It was estimated to be only 6 to 8 of the total investments, as compared to 35 to 45 per cent of the automobile industry. This meant most of the investments and expenditures would remain in the country, with little foreign currency impact.
11. The expenditure by foreign and national tourists would be spread over a wide variety of business, big and small. For example, excluding air transport, for every 100 units spent in the country the breakdown was estimated to be:

| | | | |
|---|---|---|---|
| Lodging | —— | 30—35 | per cent |
| Food and beverages | —— | 20—25 | per cent |
| Handicrafts | —— | 10—15 | per cent |
| Local transportation | —— | 10 | per cent |
| Shopping, guides, entertainment etc. | —— | 20—25 | per cent |

12. The tourist expenditure within the country is almost always equivalent to cash... This means immediate cash flow as compared to financing of conventional export products.

We were amazed to find this hidden and, to us, unknown jewel but our biggest surprise, what really made it unique, was the way the product is consumed.

How so? Well, traditionally p [products, be they industrial...or agricultural...consumer goods... or others, regardless of where they are produced, must be shipped and delivered for their use or consumption where the purchaser or client resides.

This means packaging, transporting, distributing and servicing the product, ......

Tourism in this respect is unique because the consumer

must displace himself along with his money, to his destination be it for... any of the myriad tourism products.

This makes tourism an incredibly agile and flexible tool for economic and social development...agriculture can be developed and is limited in its scope to the availability of sun, water, and climate among others. Mining can be developed where the resource is found. Industry tends to concentrate in or near the large centers of consumption, where it finds the needed infrastructure, energy, technicians, suppliers etc.

Tourism, on the other hand, given its enormous variety of segments, for all tastes and budgets, can truly be developed almost anywhere there is something of interest to do or enjoy.

To make a longer story slightly shorter, the Mexican Government concluded that if tourism had grown so well and so consistently, with little, if any, encouragement what it would not do with some help and support in planning, financing, promotion, facilitation and political and budgetary backing."

The problem with tourism however is that it is a multi-dimensional activity and its impact is not easily seen. The WTTC has identified about thirty activities, which are at the tourism business, but we commonly talk about only 5/6 of them. WTTC has therefore differentiated between 'travel and tourism industry' and 'travel and tourism economy'. By travel and tourism industry we refer to those activities commonly associated with travel and tourism like transport, accommodation and catering. Travel and tourism economy, on the other hand expresses the impact of travel and tourism in its flow through effects across the wider economy. Using an accounting method called the Tourism Satellite Account now can identify the wider effects. WTO explains TSA as follows: "Tourism satellite Account (TSA) does not have anything to do with outer space or rocket ships. Tourism for example, includes part of agriculture sector because farmers produce food for the tourists. It includes part of manufacturing, construction sector relating to building of tourism infrastructure. It also includes big part of transport and telecom industries...".

A TSA runs along side national accounts, drawing from each sector that has any tourism component without disturbing the total. It results in figures that measure tourism 'true contribution to GDP and allows tourism to be accurately compared to other economic sectors in national accounting. Under the auspices of the United Nations and WTO' many nations of the world have adopted TSA with telling effects about the impact of tourism. The difference is shown by the estimates of WTTC using this method—

**Percentage Contribution of Tourism**

| | | *World* | *India* |
|---|---|---|---|
| Contribution to GDP— | TT Economy | 10.7 | 5.3 |
| | TT Industry | 4.2 | 2.5 |
| Contribution to Employment— | TT Economy | 8.0 | 5.8 |
| | TT Industry | 3.1 | 2.9 |

This is far in excess of WTO's modest estimate of contribution of 3-5 per cent of GDP from the tourism sector. By 1998 tourism had overtaken all other categories of international trade, including automotive products, petroleum, textiles, and telecommunication. With about $ 4 trillion in total output, it is the biggest industry of the world. During the last 15 years, international tourism receipts has grown 1.5 per cent faster than the growth in world GDP and employment creation has also been 1.5 times faster than the world average. The future projections are also very impressive. According to WTO projections, the international arrivals will touch 1.6 billion by 2020 and the receipts will be $2000 billion. This figure could be much more because at present only about 7 per cent of the people who are capable of travelling are actually travelling.

How this phenomenal boom in tourism came about is a fascinating story. In 1950, tourism as an economic activity was hardly noticed. The global arrivals were 25.3 million and the total receipts a bare $2.1 billion. Between 1960 and 1970 it increased two and half times and has almost doubled every decade thereafter. Between 1970 and 2000 the numbers have increased tenfold.

Such remarkable growth was made possible by a variety of factors, like the changed safety perception after the end of the Korean War and the Vietnam War, changed geo-political situations like the break up of the Soviet Union and emergence of the Eastern Europe, economic upturn generally in the world and particularly the rise of the 'Asian Tigers', dismantling of borders and formation of the European Union etc. But perhaps no other factor contributed to this growth more than the growth in the civil aviation sector. This was also the era of unbelievable technological developments in civil aviation. It is no co-incidence that the period of biggest growth in tourism was also the period of introduction of jet propelled, wide-bodied aircraft making travel faster, quicker and safer. Changes in aviation technology widened the horizon of man's dreams and capabilities to travel. Civil aviation, more than any other factor changed the nature of tourism in the world. And it is predicted that in the future, technological developments in civil aviation will be a major influence shaping the trend of tourism developments.

While planning tourism, it is essential to understand the future trends and issues that will shape the future. The main influences have been summed up in the following categories—

1. Socio-demographic changes;
2. Changes in consumer behaviour and tastes;
3. Technological changes;
4. Human resource development;
5. Concern for sustainable development.

The 'money rich, time poor' syndrome characterizes the modern traveller. There are more two-income families and more elderly people are travelling than they did before. More people are now taking more than one vacation a year but have shorter duration. Because they travel often, they are more discerning about the services expected and look for new experiences in their travel rather than the usual travel itinerary. The countries are competing with each other in creating 'unique' experience for the traveller—an area where the NE has a natural advantage.

But the most important influence is of technology. Technology has an all-pervasive influence on human lives. It is fast changing, and as it is said, each new development compounding the speed and capability of the technology that came before it. Information technology has changed the dimension and structure of travel and tourism business. Sometimes back Bill gates was reported to have spoken strongly about tourism being one of the key sectors for attention in the 21st Century, because he thought tourism was one of the major users of IT. Now reportedly half the scheduled international Journeys are made through e-ticket. A person in New York can have a virtual reality walk through Taj Mahal in his bedroom, book his ticket and pay for it, get immigration clearances using biometric devices, transact all his business in the hotel—all using one smart card only.

Information today is power. More information, it is said, is being produced since the 1970s than was since the beginning of civilization. Information management is an art and in tourism, a major component of marketing strategy.

The impact of technological developments is the crucial issue we need to take note of and prepare in time to meet the consequences. In his Somnath Chib memorial lecture in 1999, Lord Marshall then Chairman of British Airways, had pointed to a few issues, which would be important in the future. First, the technology of flying. The satellite based Future Air Navigation System (FANS) would have the effect of ironing out the world's airways, so that we can fly in straight lines, thus reducing journey time and improving operational efficiency. The industry, it was estimated, would save $10 billion in annual cost saving which would be a great boost at the time that the industry is passing through a tough time. However the nations will have to implement satellite navigation and communication system, which is costly.

Second is the question of technological developments in aircraft manufacturing and further progress in supersonic flights. "We are much more likely to see" he stated "the airframe manufacturers moving on to the concept of mass hypersonic transport outside the earth's atmosphere, turning the trip between Delhi and London into a short-haul experience."

The implications of such developments are obvious. Any country, which hopes to be in the race to partake of the great economic opportunities, opened up by travel and tourism must device strategies to provide a totality of services to the consumer in tune with what technology has made possible. Three areas seem to be crucial components of such a strategy. First, the air corridors are naturally going to be very congested and crowded. Efficient and safe management of the air space is going to be the primary need of the future. Every country must invest heavily in futuristic technology. Fortunately, access to technology is fairly democratic and easy, but it comes at a cost.

Second, as airframe technology is also changing fast, most countries, particularly those, which depend on national carriers, have to invest constantly to acquire the latest technology for passenger comfort and safety.

Third, we have to think of totality of services. An efficient flight experience can be totally ruined by inept and inefficient ground handling and services. As the passenger traffic in the world is expected to double and triple within the next few years, the airport terminal facilities, support services, surface access systems, hotel accommodation—all these will have to keep pace. The ideal synergy between civil aviation and tourism implies a situation where the future strategic planning of each sector takes into account the totality of this scenario.

In such a scenario, developing countries like India may find themselves in very serious disadvantage. One major characteristic of the present technological revolution is that technology is changing very fast, and as has been said, each new development compounding the speed and capability of the one that came before it. Acquiring technology becomes more expensive than it was before.

The change in technology also underscores the importance of HRD in any strategic planning for travel and tourism. It goes without saying that it is not the technology as such, but the human capability behind the technology that gives strength to a nation. When technology changes so fast, HRD also becomes a costly proposition. Training has to be continuous and continuously updated. Countries trying hard to find enough resources to provide basic literacy to its population may find it extremely difficult to provide the resources for HRD in travel and tourism.

It was predicted that the process of globalisation, technological developments, and liberalized trading regime would lead to intense competition and ultimately result in change in the organization of travel and tourism business. Global alliances with integrated air services have already become a major pattern of airline business in the world. We have to take note of this development and its implications for the future of our own airlines.

It should also be kept in mind that tourism is not an end in itself. It is only a means to an end, which is human welfare. Therefore there is great concern about the ill effects of unsustainable tourism practices and even consumer movement is growing against such destinations, which flout sustainable norms.

I am mentioning these issues to underscore the point that tourism is a serious business, needs professional planning and management. If we want to be part of the revolution, our strategy for product development, marketing and infrastructure development must take into account these global developments.

It is also pertinent to mention two aspects of this growth. First, tourism growth has not helped redistribution of income among the countries. The World Development Report mentions that during the period that this phenomenal growth took place, 60 countries of the world were getting steadily poorer. Secondly, 50 per cent of the arrivals and about 50 per cent of the receipts are confined to top 10 countries, mostly developed, except that recently has made an inroad into this citadel.

> The recent developments also have seen fierce competition among nations. To take advantage of the tourism boom, we have to evolve continuously changing strategy, take planned and coordinated steps, and provide tourism a priority place in our planning. India, for example, has grown from 17,000 tourist arrivals and Rs. 7.7 crore in foreign excange earnings in 1950 to 2.67 million arrivals and Rs. 14,000 crore in earnings. But we remain in the static position in world rankings because other countries have made even faster progress and have overtaken us. Comparative growth rates of some of our neighbours illustrate this point—

| | *Av. Annual growth rate* | *Arrivals* | |
|---|---|---|---|
| | *1980—1997* | *1980* | *1997* |
| World | 04.56 | | |
| China | 11.93 | 3.5 m | 23.7 |
| Thailand | 08.31 | 1.8 m | 7.2 m |
| Singapore | 05.66 | 2.5 m | 6.5 m |
| Indonesia | 14.40 | 0.5 m | 5.1 m |
| Malaysia | 06.57 | 2.1 m | 6.2 m |
| India | 04.13 | 1.2 m | 2.37 m |

India's international tourism achievements are way behind her potential, but a few aspects of the important role played by tourism need to be highlighted. First, while India's share in world tourism is low, contribution of tourism to India's export and receipts as well as employment is high as shown by the following table—

| | World average | India | World rank |
|---|---|---|---|
| Total tourism export | | | |
| As % of total export | 12.15 | 9.5 | 31 |
| Tourism receipts | 5.2 | 11.8 | 29 |
| Numbers employed | 207.1 m | 25 m | 2nd |

*Source:* Draft 10th Plan.

Second domestic tourism plays a very significant role in Indian tourism. While the ratio of international to domestic tourism is about 1:10 in case of India it is almost 1:80. India share is about 5 per cent of the world total—

| | World | India | % share of India |
|---|---|---|---|
| International arrivals | 698 m | 2.64 m | 0.38 |
| Tourism receipts | $595 bn | $3.2 bn | 0.69 |
| Domestic tourism worldwide | 6,980 m | 210 m | 4.6 |

*Source:* Draft 10th Plan.

Domestic tourism is also growing at a very fast pace. After the disastrous effects of the September 11 events domestic tourism only helped the industry to survive and grow. Here is a message for NE tourism, which has not looked at domestic tourism with great interest.

The WTTC, on the basis of preliminary estimates using the TSA accounting system has concluded that by 2010 tourism could contribute Rs. 5,00,000 crore to GDP, 8 million new jobs, Rs. 1,30,000 crore in capital investment, Rs. 1,60,000 crore in export earnings. The possible increase over 1998 is shown below—

| | 1998 | 2010 |
|---|---|---|
| GDP | Rs. 90,500 crore | Rs. 5,00,000 crore |
| Export | Rs. 23,100 crore | Rs. 1,60,000 crore |
| Capital investment | Rs. 24,800 crore | Rs. 1,30,000 crore |

Similarly, a sample survey conducted by the Ministry of Tourism had shown the employment generating capacity of tourism. For every 10 lakh of rupees invested employment generated in some sectors were estimated as follows—

| | |
|---|---|
| Agriculture | 44.7 |
| Manufacturing | 12.6 |
| Mining and quarrying | 2.6 |
| Railways | 0.9 |
| Other transport | 13.8 |
| Tourism | 47.5 |
| Hotel and restaurant | 89.0 |

Another sample survey by the Ministry in the tourism prominent states of Rajasthan and Kerala drives home the importance of tourism in creating income and employment in the rural areas. The survey found that 90 per cent of the total income of artisan household in Rajasthan and 96 per cent in Kerala came from tourism related artisan income. For folk artists, the average per capita income during peak tourist season is nearly four times that of lean season in both the states. The survey found that tourism plays a vital role in increasing the living standard of the artisans and folk artists.

Why should Assam look at tourism as an input in economic development? Let me at this stage clarify that when I speak of Assam, the comments generally would apply to the entire NE as well.

There are two main economic reasons for looking at tourism, relevant for Assam. First, in the overall economic situation of Assam, we have to fall back on the old Ricardian theory of Comparative Advantage while looking at the options for economic strategy. Instead of duplicating what others are doing, we would be better off if we give greater weightage to things we are better at doing. Undoubtedly we have tourism potential not available with others. Secondly, unlike any other industry, every single paise spent by the tourists both domestic and foreign, is a net addition to the income of the state. Assam needs supplementary source of income generation more than anything else. He high multiplier effects of tourism activities and its strong inter-sectoral linkages, are also other points of relevance. Tourism does not require much public investment directly, can be promoted through the private sector and its net import content is also very minimal.

However, we have to be alive to our strengths and weaknesses and take them into our future planning. Normally tourism development planning does not make great distinction between domestic and foreign tourists. But Assam's planning must take into account some fine distinctions in planning for them. In respect of foreign tourists the strength of Assam lies in the product quality, which can create a unique experience that most travellers now look for, its ethnic and cultural mosaic, adventure and eco-tourism. The domestic tourist would be greatly enthused by the religious attractions, the wildlife and fauna and flora.

Infrastructure, no doubt, is a problem. First on the list is connectivity. Distance and cost of travel deter many. Second is the image. Let us have no illusions that the image of this region being a difficult place is a problem for tourism promotion. A recent sample survey of foreign tourists had put safety and security at the top of negative factors for India, followed by hygiene and hassles of road and rail journeys. All these factors are particularly true for the NE. The primary focus of tourists all over the world has changed. More people travel for leisure and hassle free enjoyment than for anything else. Just feeling, as most people do, that the image of a difficult place is not deserved is not sufficient. Concerted action is required to remove that image.

The present picture of arrivals of tourists to Assam and the NE is dismal. The figures for the last three years for Assam are—

| | *1999* | *2000* | *2001* | *% of total* |
|---|---|---|---|---|
| Domestic | 14,336 | 8,91,433 | 10,10,651 | 0.4 |
| International | 604 | 5,954 | 6,171 | 0.1 |

The figures for other states of the NE are so small that in the statistical percentage they are shown as zero. The figures for Assam, particularly sudden jump after 1999, desirable though it is, raise many statistical doubts.

Incidentally, a recent sample survey by the Ministry of Tourism shows that Assam is no. 6 in the list of Indians travelling abroad sharing 4.18 per cent of the total. While one would feel happy about the growing economic capability of the Assamese—which is in contrast to the state of the economy—obviously it means that in tourism sector also Assam has a negative balance.

The ADR identifies tourism as one of the thrust areas. If tourism has to play any role, some action agenda can be suggested. I would like only to give the broad parameters of such action and not the details.

1. The action should start with a policy, which puts tourism on higher priority than at present. This will require a change in the mindset of the policy makers. The policy must be (a) futuristic and imaginative; (b) considering the multi-disciplinary nature of tourism, the policy must not be just a sectoral policy of the tourism department but a policy of the government as a whole. This distinction is vital.
2. For getting maximum effectiveness tourism development in the NE must be an integrated one, where the strength of each state complements the others. Unfortunately, this extremely vital necessity of projecting the totality of the NE suffers from two fundamental inadequacies—lack of internal communication and lack of any organizational effort for harmonized action. The recent announcement by the Indian Airlines about a connectivity network for the NE is a very welcome development. The governments of the states and the private sector should now quickly capitalize on this and draw up marketing strategies so, that the airlines operations become

economically viable.

3. The tourism policy must be translated into concrete action plans within a definite time frame. All too often we draw up grandiose Master Plans, which remain, only on paper.
4. The NE has neglected the big boom in domestic tourism. The domestic tourist figure has reached 230 million and is growing very fast. The future of our tourism plan must be on the foundation of domestic tourism. The flow of domestic tourists will encourage development of infrastructure and more important, will slowly erase the stigma of a difficult place to visit. Tourism and peace has symbiotic relationship. As Gandhi once said, "travel is the language of peace."
5. As the resources are scarce, our pragmatic approach should be three pronged—(a) selective planning; (b) coordination with other departments; and (c) partnership with the private sector. Let me briefly explain each.
6. The ADR has identified a resource need of Rs. 7,900 crore for the next five years for the hotels, trade and restaurants sector. Though actual tourism needs have not been identified, a big resource need may be daunting enough to inhibit any action. Our planning therefore should be based on a selective approach. There is a tendency often to take up too many small, routine and unimaginative projects, which fail to have any visible impact. The tourists can be broadly classified into three types—international, domestic i.e. national tourists from outside the region and purely local and regional tourists. The available tourism products should be identified and classified according to their importance for each of these categories. Planning should also start from the lowest level. Every district should draw up a benchmark survey of tourism potential of the area. Thereafter,

those attractions, which satisfy primarily local requirements, should be included in the district development plans. The regional attractions should be taken care of by the State Plan schemes and schemes of national and international importance should be taken up with the help of national and international agencies. Thus the available resources will be able to cover a wider area.

7. Tourism being a multi-sectoral activity, in an ideal situation, the programmes of other departments like roads, forests, culture etc. can supplement the total tourism efforts. Tourism savvy states like Kerala and Rajasthan have reaped great benefits by making it obligatory for the other departments to give priority to tourism components in their own sectoral planning. If it is done as a total policy of the government, greater resources will be available and the states will reap wider benefits than is possible by following isolated policies.

8. The other neglected component in the NE is the private sector. Tourism is primarily a private sector driven industry. Most tourism successful countries have built strong partnership with the private sector. In USA, the President chaired over a tourism planning committee. After the September 11 events in the USA the government provided millions of dollars to support the industry suffering from the effects of the events. In many other countries like Egypt, Sri Lanka government came out with packages for helping the industry affected by the aftermath. As I have said before, governments of the NE must come out with bold positive policies to enable private initiatives to grow and should discard the mentality of always looking upon profit motive as public sin. The tourism industry, on their part, should respond with collective enterprise and get away from the tendency of over dependence on government for every initiative.

9. Assam and the NE should be marketed within the country and abroad in an imaginative way. Gone are the days of general statements about the beauty of the place or its tourism attractiveness. Today tourism marketing is characterized more by IT driven micro marketing than macro descriptions. Tourists ask for specific information on their specific areas of interest. He tourism managers must be trained and equipped to handle this new competition.

10. It is also important that product quality matches the marketing claims. If the packaging of our destinations does not meet the sales slogan that would be the greatest harm done to tourism promotion. As is commonly said in marketing jargon, 'you do not get a second chance to make a first impression.'

11. What are needed to make the first impression are not grand hotels and super highways—desirable though they are. Tourists look for a friendly and efficient service without hassles, clean sheets and toilets in place of accommodation, good wayside amenities, clear road signages, proper information and guidance—things that are eminently doable without very huge resources. The Kamakhya temple can be developed as big an attraction as say, the Vaishno Devi or Tirupati with only a little imaginative, will and effort. But perhaps it will be sacrilege to talk about what keep the tourists and pilgrims away now. In a recent big religious discourse that I had the opportunity to attend in Badrinath, the Swamiji asked a very pertinent question to the assemblage—"here you come and offer so many things to God, but what do you offer to the place itself, the abode of Gods? How can you aspire for purity through lack of cleanliness?"

12. That takes me to the core of tourism business today—more relevant to the NE than anywhere else—the concept of 'sustainable tourism.' Tourism is not an

end in itself; it is only a means to the end, which is greater good of the greater numbers. Tourism is not worthwhile if it destroys the very roots on which it grows. It must not affect the cultural and natural heritage that the present generation has inherited and is obligated to leave behind for the next generation. Quite often environmentally destructive and aesthetically unpleasant construction practices for tourism development affects the beauty of the place. Governments of the NE states should consider adopting an architectural code for all its private and public constructions. Also needed is a combined strategy of the government, industry and the people to implement what is commonly called "the Global Code of Ethics" in tourism.

13. The center of sustainable tourism and for that matter of any economic activity is the people. Community participation, both in promotion of tourism and in sharing its benefits, is of great importance. Since the adoption of "Our Common Future" as an agenda of common action by the world community, and the Rio Declaration, local Agenda 21 have been adopted by numerous communities around the globe for positive action for sustainable development. We should encourage the local communities to take part in tourism by forming such Local Agenda 21 and by involving the people locally through advisory or implementation committees.

14. Sustainable tourism depends on awareness and understanding, both of the tourists and the host community. The tourist has to be educated on the cultural ethos and ecological concerns of the local community. The training of all categories of tourism managers at the cutting edge level who interact with the tourists should be an integral part of long-term strategy. Wherever mass movement of tourist takes place, an orientation center to give a first hand

knowledge about the place should be established. The training programme should include the tour operators, the travel agents, guides, taxi drivers, hotel boys etc. such training necessarily will have to be a continuous process involving the private sector. In fact, the compulsive requirements of sustainable tourism have to be made a part of our life style. Making various folklores etc. that are part of our social existence and have a social message, a part of their education, can influence the minds of the young generation.

15. In the modern age tourism is all about service—the totality of service making a unique experience that the tourist looks for. Two Harvard professors have made this concept of service famous by explaining how the present age is the "age of experience economy" where every consumer is to be treated as a market. Tourism has therefore to train its managers to service a market of one. Human resource development therefore is a very crucial component of tourism development strategy.

The agenda can go on. It is a long process. It is a continuous process evolving with the experience of progress. The process is by no means unmanageable in the NE scenario. It only requires an understanding and a will to do it.

While talking of tourism in India it is tempting to quote Mexican poet Octavio Paz's words—

> "On the Veranda of Cecil Hotel
>
> Miss Penelope (canary coloured hair, woollen stockings and walking stick)
>
> has been saying,
>
> for thirty years, "oh India"
>
> Country of missed opportunities"

It applies to Assam and the NE as well. It is now time for action.

# 8

# North East Looking East—Role of Tourism*

When the Prime Minister of India recently flagged off the ASEAN car rally at Guwahati, he had flagged off more than a race. This event was symbolic of the great expectations and optimism of the people about new economic opportunities through linkages to the 'Look East' policy of the government. The 'Look East' policy envisages major opportunities for development of the NE region through 'trade led growth' strategy. The External Affairs Minister, Shri Natwar Singh outlined this strategy—"the Northeast has to adopt a trade-led growth strategy as it is through the trade route that the region can unshackle itself from the evils of poverty, unemployment and economic backwardness....The North-east is the gateway to Southeast Asia and it is in this part of India that efforts for greater Indo-Asean economic integration have to start."[1]

The optimism about open natural borders to the east triggering off much needed economic push in the region sometimes divert attention from the ground realities. Such economic integration of the Northeast with ASEAN will mean that the Northeast will more directly become part of the globalization process than hitherto. The breaking down of barriers to flow of goods, services and people, it is expected, will reduce costs of transportation. But as is well known by

* Published in 'Seminar,' June 2005 under the Caption "Tourism Prospects."

now, globalization is not an unmixed blessing, nor does it bring benefits automatically. As Joseph Stiglitz[2] puts it succinctly—"Globalization can be a force for good... Globalization has helped hundreds of millions of people attain higher standards of living, beyond what they, or most economists thought imaginable....Even so, the countries that have benefited the most have been those that took charge of their destiny and recognized the role government can play in development rather than relying on the motion of a self-regulated market that would fix its own problems."

If the region wishes to be a winning player in the open trade regime, it will have to brace itself to face many economic issues,—like improving productivity, strengthening marketing and streamlining infrastructure. The old Ricardian theory of 'Comparative Advantage' props up again and again as a suitable starting point of economic strategy for the Northeast and 'tourism' stands out as one sector where the region has distinct comparative advantage.

While prescribing tourism as an important input in the development strategy to pull the region out from its chronic underdevelopment, it is relevant to look at the nature of the economic ailment itself.

**Some Features of the Economic Scenario in the NE**

Within its apparent geographical compactness, there are wide variations in socio-economic situations in the states of the Northeast. Therefore generalization about the economic situation of the NE as a whole will be inaccurate. A general assessment of the economic situation of any state must also take into consideration issues like sectoral balances, income and employment generating measures, resource position, productivity and capital output ratios, nature of infrastructure development, investment opportunities and so on. In planning a development strategy, the socio-political issues of the area are also crucial parameters. However, we will briefly examine only those features of the economic situation in the region which substantiate the thesis that tourism can and should play an important role in the economic planning of the region in the context of the trade led growth and 'look east' policy.

*1. General Deceleration in the Economy*

The most striking feature of the economic development of the region has been a general downturn in economic performance compared to other states in the last few decades. It is reflected in the rate and pattern of growth of Net State Domestic Products (NSDP) and per capita income of the population. Dr. Gulshan Sachdeva[3] points out that "while the national economy is growing fast after initial contraction, the economies of the region are slowing down. In the decade of eighties growth rates in the North-Eastern Region were lower than the national growth rates. In the last few years the gap between national growths and regional growth rates has further widened." In 1999-2000 the per capita GDP of the region was Rs 7234 against the all-India average of Rs.10561.[4]

No doubt the situation differs from state to state but the performance of the biggest economy in the region—Assam—is often cited, indirectly though, as an argument for more opening of trade and links to the east. At the time of Independence and at the beginning of planned development in the country, Assam's per capita income was 4 per cent higher than the national at constant prices. By 1998-99 it was 41 per cent below the national average at current prices and 45 per cent below at 1980-81 prices. "What is even more alarming," states the Assam Development Report[5] "is that the gap is growing. Between 1980 and 1990, per capita income at 1980-81 prices grew by 20 per cent in Assam compared with 40 per cent for all-India. Between 1980 and 1998 per capita income in Assam grew by 10 per cent compared with 39 per cent for all India....Assam's economy decelerated in the 1990s." It is very significant that this was the period of good growth for most states spurred by economic liberalization measures. Not surprisingly, many in the NE feel that the closure of the region's trade with the South and East of Asia after independence has a correlation with the economic deceleration in the region.

### 2. *Higher Unemployment and Poverty*

Naturally, the stagnation in economic activities is reflected in the human development indicators for the region. For almost all the states of the region the percentage of people below poverty line is substantially higher than the national average. The unemployment figures are also higher than the national average—the position of Assam again being alarmingly high. One estimate[6] shows that the percentage of unemployment among the youths of 15-29 age groups has increased in Assam from 3.01 in 1983-84 to 19.25 in 1993-94 against the all India figure of 6.46 per cent that year

### 3. *Distorted Sectoral Growth*

As is to be expected, neither industry nor agriculture has shown any significant growth during this period. In Assam, for example, in the 1990s the growth rate of agriculture slowed down to 1.6 per cent from the already low figure of 2.1 of the earlier decade. Lower productivity of these sectors is compounded by disproportionate growth of the service sector. The tertiary sector has become unduly inflated[7] as the states tend to look to the public sector to accommodate the growing unemployed. This leads to cascading effects of lower productivity of investment, lower income generation in the economy resulting in reduced capital and development expenditure and therefore a continuing vicious cycle of underdevelopment. The resulting fiscal mismatch has found most of the states in serious financial distress and debt servicing has become one of the biggest components of the state expenditure. It increased from Rs. 733.34 crore in 1980 to Rs. 11,351.39 crore in 2001 in Assam and the fresh borrowing was almost eaten up by the interest payments. The Committee on Fiscal Reform set up by the Government of Assam pointed out that[8] "out of a total amount of Rs. 4,977.62 crore of un-earmarked fund in Assam's 9th Five Year Plan as much as Rs. 4,112.76 crore will be spent on salaries and establishment, constituting 82.62 per cent." The fact that 48.41 per cent of the earmarked fund also is spent on salaries and establishment should cause serious concern.

#### 4. *'Unbalanced Economy'*

Prof. Sachdeva[9] has pointed out that the states of the region import food items worth about Rs. 2000 to 2500 crore annually. That a primarily agrarian and predominantly rural economy of the region should depend so heavily on outside for primary food items reflects the weakness of the economic planning strategy. This weakness is further compounded by the fact that most of the export items of the region are primary resource based products like tea, petroleum products, plywood etc. It is in this scenario that tourism stands out as a very viable option.

#### 5. *Lack of Private Sector Investment*

Because of unsuitable geo-political situation and the constraints of distance from markets, additional investments in income generating projects in the region has been insignificant. As a result additional resource mobilization efforts by the states through excise, taxes, duties etc. are hampered. The share of the region in all-India value of factory output[10] is only 0.8 per cent and share in all-India investment in the factory sector is only 0.7 per cent.

### Why Tourism in Trade-Led Growth?

It is apparent that the region as a whole needs a big push or a kick start to put the economy on the path of development. Looking east provides an opportunity to overcome problems of distance from markets. Tourism provides a marketable product which does not depend on raw materials from outside. In a similar situation of economic doldrums in the 80s Mexico stepped out of the traditional models of economic growth to depend on tourism as an important input. This strategy showed remarkable results. Outlining the experience, the then Planning Minister of Mexico summed[11] up that tourism was relevant because—

- Agriculture and manufacturing are location specific. But tourism can be promoted and developed almost anywhere. It is therefore an ideal tool for decentralized regional development.
- It provided infinite product possibilities—anything under the sun if properly packaged and marketed—such as culture, heritage, nature, sun and beaches, cruises, business, convention, spirituality, adventure, sports, ethnicity and so forth. The benefits are more spread out and not centered around urban centers as in the case of most industries.
- Being a personal service it is hard to automate and therefore labour intensive.
- The foreign import component of investment in tourism is very low. In Mexico as a whole it was estimated to be 6-8 per cent as against 35-45 per cent of automobile industry. In case of Northeast the component would be even neglible. The tourist expenditure within the country is almost always equivalent to cash. It has therefore advantage over traditional exports in respect of immediate cash flows.
- The multiplier effect of tourism is very large. The ripple effects are widespread and the benefits are shared by an incredibly large number of service providers, like lodgings, food and beverages, handicrafts, local transportation, guides, shopping, entertainment, photography. In the total range of services many of the service providers are not visible at all.

These are only some illustrative examples and all the observations are relevant to the Northeast. The employment intensity of tourism in the Indian context was demonstrated by an oft quoted sample survey of the Ministry of Tourism.[12] According to this survey, for every million rupees invested, at 1985-86 prices, the comparative employment generation in some of the sectors are as follows—

| | | |
|---|---|---|
| • Agriculture | — | 44.7 |
| • Manufacturing | — | 12.6 |
| • Mining and quarrying | — | 2.6 |
| • Railways | — | 0.9 |
| • Other transport | — | 13.8 |
| • Tourism | — | 47.5 |
| • Hotels and restaurant | — | 89.0 |

Another recent survey by the Ministry[13] shows the impact of tourism on local level employment—"about 96 per cent of the total income of artisan household in Kerala and 90 per cent in Rajasthan comes from tourism related income. The study also indicates that tourism plays a vital role in enhancing the standard of living of the artisan families....As regards Folk Artists their average per capita income during the peak season is nearly four times that in the lean season....Share of female employment is the highest in the lower income segment of the artisan households."

**'Paradise unexplored':** The tourism potential of the Northeast has not been fully exploited. The Ministry of Tourism therefore calls the region the 'paradise unexplored.' Global tourism has been booming and the future projections show that this trend will continue. The new generations of travellers who are 'money rich and time poor' are increasingly looking for unique experiences. More and more people are looking at tourism as less of a journey and more of an experience—a phenomenon being called the emergence of the 'experience economy'.

For these new and growing breed of tourists the Northeast with its variety and uniqueness holds immense attraction. The rich natural beauty and its diversity, exotic cultural and ethnic mosaic, flora and fauna and the serenity of the virgin, unexplored eco-systems provides possibilities of a totally different experience for the tourists.

**Why Look East?**

The rationale for trade led growth strategy for the

Northeast integrated to the 'look east' policy has been well explained. The land locked Northeast, it is explained, is ideally placed to link India to the ASEAN both in geographical and commercial sense. Northeast also has very strong cultural and historical linkages with the east, which could be exploited to forge economic cooperation.

So far as tourism is concerned such an approach comes out of India's tourism experience of the last decade. This was a decade of good growth thwarted by continuous crisis—the Gulf War, the nuclear explosion and subsequent economic sanction, Kargil War, terrorist attacks on the Parliament, the Gujarat Earthquake, the Afghan War and the Iraq War, just to mention a few. The infamous 'advisories' issued by the national governments in Europe and USA—the countries from where most of the tourists come—continuously affected the tourism flow to India. Globally, in the first three years of the new millennium, tourism saw many ups and downs. The wars and the 9/11 incidents as well as the SARS affected tourism growth adversely. In almost fifty years since the World Tourism Organisation started keeping tourism statistics, the tourism growth had shown negative results only three times and two of them came during the first three years of the new millennium.

One of the lessons learnt during this time was that in periods of crisis, regional tourism and domestic tourism is the mainstay of the industry. Unfortunately, Indian tourism depends heavily on the long haul tourists of the west. Whereas globally the ratio of interregional to regional tourism is 20: 80, in case of India it is almost the exactly the other way round. The marketing strategy of the Ministry of Tourism is now looking at new markets for the tourism products and this search is aligned with the 'Look East' trade policy.

Such a policy shift is particularly relevant and important for the Northeast. Because it is situated so far away from the main entry points of the western tourists, Northeast is at a disadvantage in attracting foreign tourists from the west.

This is reflected in the negligible tourist flow to this region. In 2002 out of about 5.8 million visits to the states (by 2.75 m tourists), the Northeast received only about 22,000. If the figures of Sikkim are excluded, all the other seven states of the Northeast accounted for only 12,000 visits.

Looking to the East is fortunately a very natural marketing option for the Northeast. By 2020 the Asia Pacific region will be the second largest tourist generating market in the world. The world tourism projection shows that by 2020 this region will generate 405 m of the total 1,561 m tourists. These countries have continuous geographical land links with the Northeast. China is already vigorously developing tourism in its southern provinces to take advantage of this outbound tourists market of the region. These areas have cultural, historical and ethnic links with the Northeast. The tourism marketing strategy of the Northeast should focus on these links to establish a natural flow of people within the region including the Northeast.

In such a strategy it will be of crucial importance to develop access to this region. Presently in the western tourist dominated scenario, access to the Northeast is always seen as a constraint. While air access will have to be developed as a sine qua non of tourism development strategy, fortunately, the Asian Highway project is looming in the horizon as a great opportunity for the region. The Asian Highway can, if properly planned and integrated, change the tourism scenario of the region completely. The Asian Highway proposes to cover 90,000 km in 25 countries, of which 40,000 km will be international routes and 50,000 km regional routes. ESCAP, which is spearheading the project, recognizes excellent tourism potential of the Asian highway. ESCAP has already undertaken survey to identify the potential and the possible bottlenecks so that timely action can be taken to remove them.

Here is a golden opportunity for the Northeast to exploit. The plan of action for the Northeast with the objective of using the Asian Highway as its link to the East, could be, among others—

- The international route touches only a part of the Northeast. Therefore integrated feeder communication links should be developed through the national and state planning processes, in consultation with ESCAP. This will require quick coordination among the states and identification of suitable implementing agency.
- A comprehensive tourism potential survey should precede the planning of the routes to form feeder to the Asian Highway. Among other things, the routes planned should be able to serve and promote the most important tourism destinations.
- Tourism cannot be developed in a vacuum. It requires social and economic infrastructure for proper growth. As a first step of planning, a survey of the infrastructure gaps should be undertaken. Thereafter the projects should be prioritized on their overall importance in the trade led growth strategy. One major component for tourism should be development of wayside amenities along the Asian Highway and the feeder routes. In Japan a concept of community based tourism and wayside facilities called "Michi-no-eki" has proved immensely successful. Under this scheme, the facilities are community run with partnership of the private sector. The centers not only provide facilities, they also work as outlets for local handicraft and handloom products, and showpiece local culture, cuisine etc. Such involvement leads not only to better economic benefits for the people, but also ensures better visitor experiences.

If the very high expectations of the 'looking east' policy unleashing economic opportunities through tourism is to become a reality, the Northeast must first make an assessment of its own comparative advantage and then plan strategy based on such assessment. The South Asian Growth Quadrangle of Bangladesh, Bhutan, India and Nepal (BBIN) will touch the Northeast also directly. The Asian development Bank (ADB) has explored these growth possibilities with its

South Asia Sub-regional Economic Cooperation (SASEC) initiative. Under this initiative, the main tourism strengths of the region have been identified as (i) sustainable ecotourism and (ii) Buddhist circuit.

In both the areas the advantage of the Northeast is apparent. The SASEC concept of the Buddhist Circuit is in fact very comprehensive. It goes beyond the traditional circuit of places where Lord Buddha lived, meditated, attained enlightenment and parinirvana. It covers places of living Buddhism like Ladakh, Sikkim and Arunachal (Towang). Art, culture and archaeology of Buddhism are also integrated to the total Buddhist Circuit concept. A significantly large number of tourists from the Asia Pacific region are Buddhists and therefore these attractions may open up interest in the Northeast.

**What Needs to be Done?**

Unfortunately what is obvious is not always immediately perceived. It seems to be the case of tourism in the Northeast. In spite of such obvious advantages, tourism has not played any effective role in the economic planning of the region nor does its growth inspire any confidence. A look at the statistics will make it clear that the unique tourism resources have not been properly exploited. India itself is far away from realizing its true tourism potential. But the figures for the NE compared to the national figures are insignificant. The arrival figures of tourists both domestic and international make this abundantly clear.[14]

| | *1999* | *2000* | *2001* | *2005* |
|---|---|---|---|---|
| Arunachal Pradesh | 1008/48 | 9932/2044 | 6349/ 323 | 305/289 |
| Assam | 14336/604 | 891433/5954 | 1010651/6171 | 2467652/10782 |
| Manipur | 97523/277 | 105167/429 | 76527/183 | 94299/316 |
| Meghalaya | 159730/1971 | 169929/2327 | 178697/2390 | 375901/5099 |
| Mizoram | 27139/216 | 28221/235 | 28771/152 | 44715/273 |
| Nagaland | 21041/119 | 13272/451 | 9946/920 | 17470/883 |
| Sikkim | 138785/8554 | 143105/10409 | 203306/31028 | 151744/16523 |
| Tripura | 246507/335 | 231902/0 | 254912/0 | 216330/2677 |
| *All India* | *190671014/5832105* | *22106941/5893542* | *234200935/5427366* | *390466880/9939782* |

The total number of approved hotels and the room capacity also shows the poor state of infrastructure.[15]

*(2005)*

| | *No. of approved hotels* | *No. of rooms* |
|---|---|---|
| Arunachal Pradesh | | |
| Assam | 4 | 272 |
| Manipur | — | — |
| Meghalaya | 1 | 50 |
| Mizoram | 1 | 28 |
| Nagaland | | |
| Tripura | | |
| Sikkim | 1 | 28 |

It is quite possible that the figures suffer from deficiencies in statistical compilation. So far hotels are concerned, it is quite likely that most of the accommodation is in the unorganized sector and do not come under the purview of the government. In either situation one cannot escape the conclusion that the state of affairs is far from satisfactory.

There is much to be done. If tourism development is not taken up on priority and in a planned manner with some urgency it is quite possible that instead of tourism providing an economic push, in a liberalized atmosphere, the region may suffer from reverse flow. In tourism as elsewhere if the goods cannot meet the competition, the outflow may overtake inflow. Some of the areas in which action are to be taken to make tourism an effective tool of development, have already been mentioned. We can, by way of illustration mention a few initiatives urgently needed at the macro level.[16]

**Perception:** It is essential to start with a correct perception about the role of tourism in the economic development of the region. Unfortunately, in spite of its comparative advantage in this area, tourism is not perceived as an important economic activity. The first task of the governments should be to create awareness about the place of tourism in general and of sustainable tourism in particular in the socio-economic planning of the region. But such awareness creation efforts can start only when the governments themselves are convinced of tourism's importance and provide it due priority in the planning process.

**A Definite Policy:** Most of tourism planning in the region appears to be ad hoc. It is essential to move away from such ad hoc approach to draw up definite plans of action, charting out the future directions clearly. Every state must bring out a pragmatic tourism policy not couched in general terms but clearly defining an implementable action plan. It should indicate the government's commitment to sustainable tourism, the place assigned to tourism in the broad development planning, the role of government and of the other key players. The policy should identify the organizational pattern to implement the policy and a system of monitoring and accountability.

Tourism policy would remain the wish list of the tourism department alone unless it reflects total government commitment. Tourism being a multi-dimensional activity depends on the involvement of many other agencies for its success. Other departments like roads, culture, and forest and so on can play a very important role in the development of the total tourism product. For achieving maximum coordination, institutional arrangements should be put in place.

**The Starting Point-domestic Tourism:** Domestic tourism plays a very key role in Indian tourism. Against the average ratio of about 7 domestic tourists per one foreign tourist in the total picture internationally, in India the ratio is about 1:100. In absolute terms the figure of total domestic tourists is about 300 million against 3 million foreign tourists. The NE has a very insignificant share of this huge number of tourists who contribute to employment and income generation in other states. Movement of domestic tourists will slowly improve the image of the place and the demand created will lead to development of essential infrastructure. This process will then facilitate movement of foreign tourists.

**A Broad NE Perspective in Planning:** Because of its geographical position tourism planning of the NE states, whether aimed at the domestic or the foreign tourists, would be most attractive and cost effective if based on an integrated NE perspective. Globally also, regional cooperation in tourism has been the new strategy and many institutional arrangements for such regional tourism have developed. The attractions of the different states, rather than competing, should supplement each other and enhance the total attraction of the region. Unfortunately this vital necessity of projecting the totality of NE tourism suffers from two fundamental inadequacies—

1. Poor internal communication between the states. The road communication is arduous and time consuming. Air communication of late has improved, but is not yet tuned to tourism requirements. Coordinated planning of tourism for the NE is possible only when the internal communication by air becomes efficient and reliable.
2. Lack of organizational set up. There is no organizational set up that can harmonies action for projecting NE tourism as a whole. Prospective tourists who want to visit and sympathetic entrepreneurs who want to market the NE find it exasperating to draw up an integrated schedule for the whole region. There is too much of dependence on the government and too little incentives for the private sector to enable them to play an effective role. If tourism in the NE has to grow, a common platform of all the states, involving the government and the non-governmental agencies should be immediately set up.

These are only a few illustrative areas where action has to start on a priority basis. The action agenda is long because the Northeast has a lot to catch up with. Human resource development, creating institutional arrangements for people's participation, looking at ways to harness greater resources for tourism, creating public-private partnership are some of the issues which will demand attention as tourism grows.

"Even a five thousand mile journey must start with the first step" says an old Chinese proverb. There is a long journey ahead of the Northeast as it tries to look eastward. A beginning has to be made soon.

## REFERENCES

1. Goswami, Roopak, 'Racing towards a dream'. *The Telegraph. Guwahati,* 8 December 2004.
2. Stiglitz, Joseph, Globalization and its Discontents. *Penguin.* New Delhi, 2002, p. 248.
3. Sachdeva, Dr. Gulshan, "North–Eastern Economy: Past Policies, Present Realities and Future Possibilities," unpublished paper presented in the Seminar on 'North-East: Challenges and Response' at Nehru Memorial Museum, New Delhi, 19-21 December 2002.
4. Confederation of Indian Industries. (CII) 'India-Asean Economic Integration—The North Eastern Gateway'. 2004, p. 8.
5. Planning Commission. Government of India, Assam Development Report, 2002, p. 1.
6. Das, H.N. "The Present Financial Crisis in Assam". *Dialogue.* Vol. 4, No. 1, 2002, p. 95.
7. Bhattacharjee, Dr. P.R. "The problem of ensuring Financial Efficiency in the North-Eastern States". *Dialogue.* Vol. 4, No. 1, p. 66.
8. Das, H.N., *op. cit.,* p. 88.
9. Sachdeva, Dr. Gulshan, *op. cit.*
10. CII., *op. cit.,* p. 10.
11. Savignac, Antonio. Quoted in 'Indian Tourism Beyond the Millennium' by M.P. Bezbaruah, Gyan Publishing House, New Delhi, 1999, p. 125.
12. Bezbaruah, M.P., *op. cit.,* p. 123.
13. Ministry of Tourism. *Tourism Statistics,* 2002, p. 117.
14. Ministry of Tourism. 2001, *op. cit.,* p. 56.
15. Ministry of Tourism. 2001, *op. cit.,* pp. 59-84.
16. The following section draws heavily from author's presentation "Sustainable Tourism and Economic Development of the NE" in the Seminar organized by ICSSR, NEHU in Shillong in October 2003.

# 9

# Paradise Unexplored*

Sitting on the bank of the Brahmaputra, Mahatma Gandhi once wrote that the fabled Thames or the grandeur of Switzerland paled into insignificance before the majestic beauty of the Brahmaputra and the robust landscape of Assam. Assam in those days comprised of most of the present day Northeast. Time passed, history changed and what was Assam and the two union territories of Manipur and Tripura at the beginning of the Republic in 1950, changed to the seven states of Arunachal Pradesh, Assam, Manipur, Meghalaya, Mizoram, Nagaland and Tripura—popularly called the 'Seven Sisters'. Then the colourful state of Sikkim joined the family to make the Northeast the most exotic and enchanting region in the country. The Northeast is 8 per cent of the total geographical area of the country, and with 98 per cent of its borders with foreign countries, is India's gateway to the East.

The Ministry of Tourism describes the Northeast as the 'paradise unexplored'. But can any phrase or word truly describe the beauty of the place? Are the colours of the rainbow sufficient to capture the myriad hues of culture, craft and ethnicity that is Northeast?

The beauty of the Northeast is its variety. It is the melting pot—cauldron, if you like—of culture, heritage and tradition. The states differ in ethnicity, topography, climate and culture.

---

* Published in "Discover India" New Delhi April 2005, under the Caption 'Heaven is here.'

Within each state again there is bewildering variety, making the Northeast always an exhilarating and unique experience. Tribal population predominates. The percentage ranges from 30 to 94 in the other states except Assam. Out of 635 tribes in the country, more than 200 are in the Northeast. They speak many languages—about 200, not counting may be another 200 dialects. Yet, in this variety there is a strong common bonding.

It is believed that the ethnic diversity can be traced primarily to five races that came to the area during different periods of history. The Austrics came from around Indo-China; the Negroids from south and southwest China; the Kiratas of Mongolian origin; the Aryans from the Gangetic plains. How the numerous tribes traversed and finally settled down in this area over a period of time is a fascinating story. So much is the strange diversity of such assimilation that some Mizos believed that they were the descendants of one of the lost tribes of Israel.

Because of such ethnic differences with the Gangetic plains, because of geographical distance and tenuous links with the rest of India through the 20 km 'chicken neck' in North Bengal, Northeast has often assumed an element of romantic mysticism. Ram Manohar Lohia, for example, called the then North East Frontier Agency, present Arunachal Pradesh, 'Urvasiam'—the veil of the dancing damsel of heaven. Such mystic aura caused misconception at times that the region is at the cultural periphery of India. Mythology, folklore and history however tell a different story of an ancient land and culture with deep connections to the Ramayana-Mahabharata traditions of India.

Mythology abounds in delectable stories of such links. The *Puranas* refer to the places and people of the region. *Kamadeva,* the god of love, burnt to ashes by the rage of *Shiva* for his audacity in trying to disturb his meditation, was reborn here in old Kamarupa. Kings and princes from this region—for example Bhagadatta from Assam and Ghototkacha from

Nagaland, fought with distinction in the Mahabharata war. Lord Krishna eloped with his consort Rukmini from this area and Parasuram, seeking atonement from his son of killing his mother was delivered of his burden here in Parasuram *kunda.* The stories are endless and the links continue throughout history down to modern days. How many states of India can boast of the feat of young Kanaklata, all of fourteen years, leading the freedom fighters with the tricolour and fearlessly falling to the British bullets? And did not Nehru call Rani Guidulu of Nagaland who fought against the British rule, his sister?

The Northeast has many "firsts" in its tourism attractions. Mowsynram near Cherrapunji is the highest rainfall area in the world. Majuli, the seat of Vaishnavite culture, is the biggest river island in the world. Loktak, in Manipur is considered to be the largest fresh water lake in the country.

The Brahmaputra is the life line of the Northeast. Like the Mekong river, it also offers tremendous tourism opportunities. Brahmaputra is also called the 'Lohit'—the red river. A very popular story relates how Usha, the daughter of the Asura king Bana, dreamt and fell in love with Aniruddha, the grandson of Krishna. Her friend, Chitralekha with her magical powers brought Aniruddha to Tezpur to the pining lover but Bana confined him in the riverine hillock, Agnigarh. Krishna came to rescue his grandson and Bana, being a devotee of Shiva invoked his help. A fierce fighting took place and blood flowed making the river red. 'Agnigarh' is still preserved as a testimony to this old story.

Along the Brahmaputra in the plains of Assam are 700 and more tea gardens spreading a green carpet. The British annexed Assam in 1826 after the treaty of Yandaboo with the Burmese but tea. was discovered even before that by one British major, Robert Bruce. The Northeast also has great oil and natural gas resources in Assam, Tripura, Arunachal Pradesh and Nagaland. Oil exploration in Assam, started in 1866 is also a legendary story. The first refinery set up in

Digboi in 1901 is one of the oldest in the world and after a hundred years is still functioning.

The region's unique bio-diversity indeed makes it a paradise for nature lovers and tourists looking for something off the beaten track. The tropical lush green forests and hills have a fresh vitality about them that set them apart. To illustrate this, a story is often related of a British forest officer who lost his walking stick in the jungles. Next day when he went looking for it, he found it sprouting—so fertile is the soil!

From the snow capped mountains of Sikkim, to the rugged hills of Nagaland, Arunachal Pradesh, Manipur, Tripura and Mizoram, the rolling meadows of Meghalaya, called the 'Scotland of the East', and the verdant plains of Assam traversed by the mighty Brahmaputra and its numerous tributaries, there is surprise at every step in the diversity of the landscape of the Northeast. No wonder the entire Northeast is dotted with a number of game sanctuaries and national parks—Namdapha National Park (Arunachal); Khangchendzongpa National Park and five game sanctuaries (Sikkim); Itangki Wildlife Sanctuary (Nagaland); Sepahijhora, Gomti, Trishna and Rowa wild life sanctuaries (Tripura); Phawngpui and Murlen National Parks and four wild life sanctuaries and a tiger reserve in Mizoram; Kaziranga, Manas, Numeri and Dibru-Saikhowa National Parks and two wildlife sanctuaries in Assam; Nokrek and Balpakram National Parks and two wildlife sanctuaries in Meghalaya. The most famous of them all is Kaziranga—habitat of the world's largest (1,700) one horned Rhino population. Kaziranga also has the world's largest population of the Eastern Swamp Deer.

Truly the Northeast is a natural habitat of a large number of exotic fauna and flora and a nature lover's delight. It is not commonly known that this region has about 900 species—or about three-fourths of all the bird diversity of India. Out of about 1,000 species of orchid varieties identified in the country about 500 rare ones are found in Arunachal Pradesh and more than 400 in Manipur.

Mahatma Gandhi once said, "Assamese women can weave fairly tales in their looms". This statement is true in all senses for the whole of the Northeast. The tribal loin loom weaving technique is unique. The weaver becomes a part of the textile—transferring the strength of the warp and the weft through movements of the waist to which the loom is tied. The exquisite designs also often tell a story. The colours and design of the shawls in Nagaland, for example, will say which tribe the wearer belongs to, what is the social status and a lot of other things. Delicate weavings in the unique Muga silk of Assam, Puans of Mizoram and Jainsems of Meghalaya, all are part of the local culture and a shopper's delight.

If textile is the artistry of the people, cane and bamboo work is a way of life. Throughout history, in their struggle for coexistence with nature, the Northeast people developed a bamboo culture –using cane and bamboo for every possible needs of daily life, weaving their imagination into the baskets of exquisite designs and craftsmanship. In inaccessible places of Arunachal Pradesh and Nagaland, even today one can see marvels of workmanship and engineering sense in long cane and bamboo bridges across rivers of swift currents. It indeed is a world beyond.

The Northeast vibrates with dances and music that reflect the community's joyous celebrations of life—vibrant, graceful and blending with nature. The world famous Manipuri dance, extolling the legends of Lord Krishna, has attained the purity of classical dance form. The graceful, ornamental Nongkrem dance of Meghalaya, the rhythmic, vigorous harvest dance, Bihu of Assam, the unique Cheraw Bamboo dance of Mizoram are just a few of hundreds of folk dance forms that echo through the hills in the quiet evenings.

The strength of the region in religious tourism has not been fully developed yet. The most famous of such attractions is the ancient Kamakhya temple, the place of Shakti worship and a world famous centre for tantric studies. Tripura has many old temples and religious places, prominent being the

Unakoti—one of largest bass-reliefs in the country and the Terracotta temple plaques at Pilak.

Yet not fully known to the world, the Northeast has some of the finest jewels of the Buddhist traditions. Sikkim is in fact an example of 'living Buddhism'—serenity and devotion permeating the fresh mountain air. It has 107 monasteries, four sacred caves blessed by Guru Rimpoche and 29 sacred lakes. Some of the finest examples of Buddhist art and tradition are to be found in the imposing monasteries of Rumtek and Pemayangtse. The Towang monastery in Arunachal Pradesh at a height of 3,400 meters, amidst resplendent scenic beauty nestling the snowcapped east Himalayan ranges, is one of largest monasteries in the country.

The Northeast is India's gateway to the East and during the Second World War, was part of the British military operations against the Japanese. The region is strewn with many war cemeteries, the most important of them being the one in Kohima where a fierce battle was fought. Amidst the poignant inscriptions on thousands of graves of soldiers who died far away from their homes is the most touching reminder,"when you go back home, tell them of us and say, for their tomorrow we gave our today." In Churachndpur in Manipur also are preserved some of the memories of the advancing INA and Netaji Subhas Chandra Bose.

But sadly, all such great potential for tourism in the Northeast still remains untapped. In 2002 out of 5.8 m visits of foreign tourists to different states the Northeast received only 20,000 and barely 1.2 million out of India's 310 m domestic tourists. There are problems in plenty. The image of the place as a difficult one is a major hurdle. Insurgency and conflict fuelled by political and economic aspirations mar the landscape. Happily many areas still remain oasis of idyllic bliss. And in most areas the common people remain traditionally hospitable and welcoming. In this turmoil Mizoram has shown the way for others. Bruised and battered by 20 years of insurgency, Mizoram today is one of the most peaceful places in India. Its new slogan—'peace pays'. And it does. Mizoram has jumped up in its human development indicators since its return to peace.

Travel, to quote Gandhiji again, is the language of peace. Growth of tourism both domestic and international, can alter the socio-political scenario of the region. Recent efforts to integrate the Northeast to the 'Look East' policy of India and the prospect of the Asian Highway linking the region to the South and East Asia have created tremendous optimism about trade led growth. A market of 500 m people is now within the reach of the Northeast. So is the prospect of a portion of 504 m outbound tourists of Asia Pacific by 2020, being lured to the region by common cultural bonds, ethnic links and the unique natural attractions . There is evidence to suggest that a trade route from Northeast India through Myanmar to China existed as early as the Kushan times. In all probability Northeast India was at the southern trail of the Silk Route And it can happen again.

To make this dream a reality, as in the rest of the country, tourism infrastructure like roads, accommodation and air connectivity will have to be improved greatly. Luckily, the air connections to the region and within the region has improved but much remains to be done to make the access easy, dependable and tourism friendly. The roads are strenuous and wayside facilities ad hoc and unorganized. Institutional arrangements for a total Northeast perspective in planning is inadequate and efforts for public—private partnership are conspicuous by their absence. Man-made hurdles like the Restricted Area permits and the Inner Line permits cause irritations and difficulties to prospective tourists. Northeast has to embark urgently on a pragmatic strategy to remove these bottlenecks.

Through the centuries, what every migrating race and every invading army coming to the region have been saying about this land sum it up all—

This land is like no other land.

# *PART III*
# REGIONAL

# 10

# Indian Tourism and European Union*

I am delighted to have an opportunity to address this elite gathering. In fact I may say that I am doubly delighted because first, tourism now seems to be "business". All my efforts in the last seven years of active association has been devoted to creating that space for tourism in India and not to consider it as an invisible that just happens. I must compliment you on your sagacity.

Secondly, and more important, tourism now seems to be good business. At this time around, world tourism is in a very optimistic mood. The last couple of years of turmoil, —of wars, terrorist attacks, SARS—saw for the first time the tourism figures dip since WTO started taking count of tourists and their spending. All the time however, the world body was of the opinion that continued economic stagnation, particularly in the USA, Germany and Japan was a greater cause of concern than occasional hiccups created by unforeseen events. But now reportedly in USA, in the third quarter of the year, the US economy expanded at an annualized rate of 8.2 per cent—the fastest for twenty years. Organisation of Economic Cooperation and Development—OECD—predicted a 4.2 per cent growth in 2004 against 2.9 this year. Happy times, it seems are here again for tourism.

Before I go into an action agenda for India-EU tourism

---

* Speech in Fourth India-EU Business Summit at New Delhi November 28-29, 2003.

cooperation it would be appropriate to briefly look at the global scenario and the lessons learnt from the last few years.

The economic impact of tourism are known and I would not like to spend time repeating them.For example, the biggest industry

GDP contribution ranging from 2 to 40 per cent;

Main source of foreign exchange earnings of 38 per cent nations;

One of the top five export earnings of 83 per cent countries;

Employment generation etc.

It grew tenfold between 1970 and 2000 from 70 m arrivals to 700 m.

And one must note that in all these the crucial difference was made by developments in Civil Aviation.

Tourism growth which was cruising along the projected path to 1.6 billlion by 2020, got a big jolt in 2001. And in the star of the show, Asia Pacific, faced in 2002 more havoc from an unknown virus than from all the sinister designs of the terrorists.

But tourism is a resilient industry. WTO never wavered from its prediction that it will come back to its growth path—and it has. The results of 2002 were better than expected. In 2001 all regions except Asia Pacific registered negative growth. In 2002, all regions except the Americas witnessed positive growth.

**What are the Salient Lessons of the Last Two Years?**

1. Uncertainty made tourists go for late bookings.'Wait and watch attitude dominated.
2. Intense competition for the reducing numbers led to cheaper rates and less expensive modes of travel. Earnings of countries dropped more than proportionately.
3. Airlines resorted to reduced capacity. It had impact on grwth when things were looking up.

4. Domestic tourism was the mainstay of tourism industry everywhere.
5. Also, more intra regional tourism than ever before.
6. Recovery was good in aggregate but not uniform. Those who managed the crisis better got advantage in the competitive scenario.
7. Tourism witnessed market repositioning everywhere. Intra regional tourism, new destinations which are easily accessible and safer, short duration tours which are less expensive dominated the marketing scenario and accordingly marketing strategies required changes. Along with marketing and promotion, countries learnt the importance of good public relations—to restore confidence about the safety of tourist in any particular destination. For example, Sri Lanka's 'Invest in Peace' campaign paid very rich dividends.
8. In any recovery plan air safety and security will be crucial. South Asia for example, depends on air connectivity heavily. It gets 75 per cent of its tourists from long haul destinations as compared to 20 per cent of the rest of the world.
9. 47 per cent of SA's arrivals are from Europe.

The crisis had, ironically a silver lining for tourism in many countries like India. In the decline of tourism they were rudely made aware of its contributions. India has benefited by way of stronger total govt. support to tourism, improvement in product quality, and its diversity, willingness to look at the problem of accessibility in a pragmatic manner, more support to the industry in relation to taxation and pricing—to name a few.

**Now Let Us Look at the Issues of Today**

The tourism issues, to be meaningful, have to be discussed against the background of totality of issues of common interest. We have to fit them into the major concerns of EU globally in general and into the framework of India-EU economic relationship. I am glad that the purpose of this session has been stated as—'focus on cooperation, and taking initiatives to increase people to people contact.' I think these are crucial issues.

One major area of EU concern is participation in the global action against poverty.The World Tourism Organisation with its headquarters in Madrid has spearheaded a project for Sustainable Tourism with Elimination of Poverty (STEP), jointly with UNDP. The project launched in Johannesburg World Summit for Sustainable Development in August 2002 is a manifestation of the basic objectives of the UN Millennium Development Goals and also of WTO's Global Code of Ethics. There are great possibilities for collaborative action to put institutional arrangements to carry the benefits of sustainable tourism to the grass-root levels.

The other area of action is in Human Resource Development. EU has some of the finest institutions for tourism human resource development. In an era of what is being called 'the experience economy' tourism development is increasingly veering towards creating unique experiences for the demanding and discerning travellers. India has excellent base for tourism human resource development and with EU collaboration could develop a regional hub of excellence in tourism HRD. In fact, some time back an excellent initiative in the form of South Asia Tourism Human Resource Development Programme was launched by EU and it had created tremendous impact. This programme basically for training of trainers in the hospitality industry was ideally suited for India and the South Asia but was suddenly withdrawn. Even now there is need for such collaboration.

The new Tourism Policy of India emphasizes the cultural and spiritual contents of Indian tourism.India is embarking on new initiatives for heritage preservation and promotion in a big way. The setting up of the Culture Fund for resource mobilization and creating public private partnership in maintenance and beautification of heritage properties are some of such efforts. EU has done some pioneering work in these areas. This could lead to useful technical collaboration.

In fact in cultural and heritage tourism EU stands out in much the same manner that does India. A recent survey by the WTO had shown that 20 per cent of the EU travellers travel only for the purpose of experiencing culture and heritage and for 60 per cent culture is a major motivation or concern. Yet why so few of them come to India which has the best to offer in culture and heritage? There is scope for collaborative efforts for marketing cultural tourism and creating greater awareness among the EU tourists. Perhaps we take our common concerns for granted. But apparently there is need for massive campaign to create awareness not only about the marketing of these products but also about the commonality of concern for culture and heritage about rediscovering ourselves.

The present situation of tourist arrivals between these regions however is very disappointing. Tourist arrivals to India from the EU countries was

821112 in 2001 in a total of 25,37,282
730466 in 2002 in a total of 23,84,364

During this time there was a decline of 11 per cent for arrivals from EU whereas the total decline in arrival was only 6 per cent. That shows that traffic from this region is more volatile. We have to go into why and what can be done to prevent it. One area for close scrutiny will of course be ease of connectivity.

These figures of arrival is insignificant compared to the potential. In the total out bound of the world, the share of Europe (of which EU would be the most predominat) has been growing in numbers—from 265 m in 1990 to 403 in 2001, with a market share of 58.2 per cent. The figure of .8 m who travel to India is too insignificant and unfortunately that too was declining in the last few years.

True, a large portion of this outbound from Europe is

regional tourists. A survey shows that stronger exchange rate of the euro has induced many travellers to travel within their own country or to take short duration breaks to nearby destinations. This should encourage travel to destinations like India where travellers can get benefit of strength of their currency.

But a disturbing fact is that the total percentage of arrivals from the region is steadily declining from 33.1 per cent in 2000 to 32.4 per cent in 2001 and 30.6 per cent in 2002. There are positive signals that this trend would be reversed now. We have to ensure that the decline was only a temporary phase related to the events of this period.

In a sense, if we talk in terms of proportionate share, in tourism we may be having an adverse terms of trade with EU. We have only very inadequate statistics of outbound tourism from India. The figures of Government of India shows that about 20 per cent of the outbound is for EU region. It is the fifth largest destination with about 3,35,000 travellers from India going to Europe. A correct appraisal may put this figure much higher. And knowing the propensity of Indian travellers to spend, it is likely that the foreign exchange outgo will be proportionately higher.

Well, I would look forward to the learned discussions. I have noted a few issue for your assessment. But I think the greatest contribution of this forum would be if we could go from the conference mode to create institutional arrangements for continuous dialogue on tourism issues—creating a platform for public private partnership.

It is a long journey. But my favourite quotation has been a Chinese saying—"even a thousand mile long journey must start with the first step". Let us take that step.

# 11

# Global Tourism and Asia*

Beginning with the tragic events of September 11, 2001 tourism in the new millennium has been affected by a string of troubles. Just as the tourism sector was recovering from the shock of 9/11, came a series of frightening terrorists attacks which shattered the confidence of already shaken travellers—in Djorba, in Mumbassa, in Cassablanca and the worst in the history of world tourism since the Second World War—Bali. The Asian region and India were particularly affected by the Afghan war, the uncertainties created by the Iraq war and the devastating effects of SARS. The impact of SARS on Asian tourism was far more extensive than it appeared at first. What damage the wars and the terrorists could not do to Asian tourism, a small and unknown virus did in a span of few months. Globally, the combination of all these factors caused ***the first dip in international tourism*** since the World Tourism Organisation (WTO) started the statistical database some fifty years back.

Many lessons have been learnt during this critical period and it maybe worthwhile to recall some of them as a guide for future action. First, the nations have learnt that pre-crisis planning should be built into the process of national tourism development plans. Honest and transparent communication was an important and effective element of crisis management strategy. Those countries which had planned earlier and were

* Written for Express Travellers and Caterers. Annual Issue. January 2004.

better prepared to meet the challenge responded quickly, withstood the shock better and recovered quicker. Therefore the process of recovery was not evenly shared among the nations.

Many national governments like USA, Egypt, France came out with immediate financial and other support for the industry. Two lessons were clear. Effective counteraction has to be initiated by the government across sectors and should not be limited to the action in the department of tourism only. Secondly, both in pre-crisis and post-crisis planning the entire tourism fraternity should be involved in partnership.

The crisis also highlighted the importance of market repositioning for India and Asia. Every crisis in recent times has shown that long haul traffic is the first to be affected. Regional tourism has become more relevant and important. Regional groups like the ASEAN have emerged as focal points for tourism interest more than before—so much so that countries like China, Japan and Korea have forged formal alliance with ASEAN by forming ASEAN+3 grouping. South Asia in general and India in particular, have tried similar strategies and India also has focussed on 'Look East' policy.

And during the worst period, domestic tourism sustained a beleaguered industry. This was the story in China, this was the experience of India and in fact of most other countries affected by drop in long haul traffic.

These years of turmoil also drove home some plain truths. First is the crucial role that civil aviation plays in tourism growth. After 9/11 aviation sector literally plunged, so did tourism. For countries like India the lesson is even more important. India gets 95 per cent of its international arrivals by air. 75 per cent of India's foreign tourists are inter-regional whereas the global average for inter-regional traveller is only 20 per cent.

Second, the last few years have shown that overall economic situation affects tourism more than anything else.

In that sense the income elasticity of tourism is very high. In the last three years the main tourist generating countries—USA, Japan, Germany for example—had been struggling with nagging economic recessions. As the year 2004 approaches, all the signs on the economic front in these countries are positive. Tourism sector is already experiencing the 'feel good' factor of the pent up demand being released. It is time for Asia and the South Asia region to put their acts together to reap the maximum benefit of this recovery.

There is no doubt that the tourism industry will bounce back to its projected growth path in the coming years. Past experiences have shown that sensitive though it is to a host of other factors, tourism is also a very resilient industry. During the Gulf war tourism growth suffered and dropped to 1.2 per cent but in 1992 jumped to 8.3 per cent. In 1999, the year of Kosovo conflict the growth was only 3.8 per cent but the very next year it rose to 7.4 per cent. After the dip in the last few years the industry can justifiably look forward to a boom period.

At the dawn of the new millennium, tourism was riding high achieving a tenfold growth since 1970. 9/11 changed all that and 2001 saw the first negative growth (–0.6) in fifty years. But even in this year Asia Pacific and Africa region were the only ones to show positive growth. By 2002 recovery process was well on and the Americas were the only region to show a negative growth. The global growth rate of 3.1 per cent was in tune with the projected growth path. Asia and the Pacific remained, according to the WTO, 'the star of the show', with highest growth rates of 5 per cent in 2001 and 7.9 per cent in 2002. China registered a growth rate of 11 per cent and Hong Kong 21 per cent. With 131 million arrivals the Asia Pacific was the most visited region of the world. WTO predicted that it would be the 'destination of the future'.

But SARS affected the region very badly and all the major destinations suffered heavily in the first-half of 2003 as can be seen from the figures below—

| | | |
|---|---|---|
| Malaysia | — | (–31%) |
| Singapore | — | (–28%) |
| Indonesia | — | (–21%) |
| China | — | (–28%) |
| Thailand | — | (–17%) |

Faced with such reverses these countries have launched massive promotional measures which are already showing results. The measures centre around following broad programmes—

1. Strengthen safety and public health awareness in tourism and assure the travellers about the safety of the destinations.
2. Engage in intensive promotional campaigns to boost up the country's image. China, for example, has embarked on a massive "China Forever" campaign and has enhanced its promotional budget substantially.
3. Organise confidence building international events to show case the country's products and capabilities. China hosted in October 2003, inspite of the uncertainties of SARS, the General Assembly of the WTO and are already launching the campaign for the "Olympics for Tourism."
4. Promote domestic tourism.
5. Build strong partnership with the private sector by providing them support and incentives.

South Asia and India also passed through ups and downs during this period. In India the arrivals dropped by (–6.6 per cent) in 2002 bringing the total arrivals to a low level of 2.35 million, even though the South Asia region as a whole showed a growth rate of 2 per cent. In 2003 so far India has reported a robust growth of 15 per cent thereby moving back to the pre-2001 figure of 2.65 million. At the threshold of 2004 one can discern a few very promising indicators for India and South Asia.

First, the crisis has spurred India, Nepal, Sri Lanka and Maldives to launch some aggressive and focussed marketing. India's 'Incredible India', Maldives' 'Sunny Side of Life', Sri Lanka's 'buy one, get one free' campaigns have created good impact.

Second, faced with series of unforeseen crisis situations the countries have shown greater attention to crisis management as an inbuilt mechanism of state policy rather than as ad hoc measures. Sri Lanka's 'Invest in Peace' campaign launched during the height of troubles is a good example of aggressive measures to restore consumer confidence.

Similarly, it is a very good trend that that India has realised the vulnerability of dependence on a few long haul markets and has been looking for new source markets. Attempts to forge tourism links with ASEAN, along with a conscious 'Look East' policy are steps in the right directions and can reap rich dividends in the long run.

It is also heartening that improvement of the product quality has received greater attention than before. Another positive development in the Indian scenario is the willingness shown by the government as a whole to give greater importance to tourism by providing more budgetary support and concessions in taxation and pricing.

Perhaps the greatest source of optimism for the future is in the willingness shown to address the problems of the civil aviation sector and a desire to put in place world class infrastructure. The Naresh Chandra Committee's recommendations for enhanced seat capacity, liberalisation in the aviation sector to provide a totality of world class flying experience, reduction in the cost of domestic flights are things that can mark the beginning of a new chapter in Indian tourism.

These positive developments may show concrete results only over a period of time. But in 2004, if the momentum of the steps to promote India can be maintained then it should be possible to maintain the 15 per cent growth rate achieved in 2003. If that happens, in 2004 India will cross the 3 million mark. Though way behind the 5 million mark we had set for ourselves for the end of the century, it would be nevertheless a good landmark.

There are however some dangers the industry may overlook in the euphoria of good arrivals this season. The media has reported that bookings have been cancelled by travel agents because air seats and accommodation both are in short supply compared to demand. The long-term implications of such a situation may be adverse. There is a lot of pent up demand in the market. India's focussed marketing may succeed in attracting a sizeable portion of this demand. But if the supply does not match, India may unnecessarily attract the tag of being a difficult destination. There is always a time gap in creating infrastructure. Therefore there is an element of urgency in looking at these areas while we go all out on our marketing.

The demand and supply mismatch in the accommodation sector may also lead to artificial hiking of prices. Unless that is avoided in collaboration with the industry, India may find itself disadvantaged in this cost conscious competitive industry. In 2004, Indian tourism industry looks promising but it requires a great amount of planned action to benefit from it. Any complacency induced by the feel good factor may be self-defeating.

# 12

# Indo-Nepal Tourism*

India and Nepal have, in respect of tourism, one striking similarity—both have tremendous potential as yet only partially realized. It is fitting therefore that in the context of bilateral cooperation, possibilities of tourism cooperation are being explored, within the broad parameters of trade. Tourism has now emerged as the biggest industry of the world and countries like India and Nepal can ignore it only at their cost. Globally tourism contributes 8 per cent of total export earnings and 37 per cent of the export in services. It is one of the top five export categories of 83 per cent of the countries of the world and is the main source of foreign exchange earnings for at least 38 per cent of the countries. Multiplier effect of tourism in job and income creations is well-known and is statistically firmly established. A sample survey in India had shown that per million rupees of investment, tourism creates more job than agriculture or manufacturing activities. The impact of tourism is more widespread and is not concentrated in any particular area. Tourism helps local crafts and art and is particularly favourable for employment of women. All these factors should make it a very useful tool for development in Nepal. Unfortunately, during the period that tourism boom occurred i.e. 1980–2000 according to the World Development Report 80 countries of the world became steadily poorer.

---

* Presented in the Seminar on "India-Nepal Relation." Observer Research Institute of Asian Studies at New Delhi, February 13-14, 2003.

Countries like India and Nepal have therefore, to take measures to take advantage of the benefits of tourism.

It is essential that the future planning of tourism take into account the influences that are likely to shape the future of tourism. There is general agreement that these issues can be grouped into the following:

1. Changing consumer behaviour and tastes;
2. Socio-demographic changes;
3. Influence of technological revolution;
4. Concern for sustainable development;
5. Human Resource Development.

The tourism profile of Nepal shows some very interesting trends, which must be kept in mind while planning for tourism in Nepal or for that matter planning any strategy for joint collaboration.

First is the fact that tourism had been for sometime the highest foreign exchange earner. In a small landlocked economy, the importance of tourism can therefore be easily appreciated. Moreover in the peculiar natural position that the country is placed in, the economic development strategy has to be based on the wider interpretation of the theory of comparative advantage, i.e., exploitation of the resources that give it an advantage over others. In fact the most important development in the twenty-first century in tourism is that consumers now look for 'unique experience' which Nepal and India can provide. During the major part of the 90s contribution of tourism to GDP was estimated to be around 4 per cent. Quite possibly this will be an underestimation because like most countries in the region, Nepal does not have a proper accounting system which can identify accurately the ripple effects of tourism activities down the economy across various sectors. The World Travel and Tourism Council had shown that there is a difference between the 'tourism industry' and the 'tourism economy'—the second is wider and encompasses possible effects of tourism activities beyond the easily perceptible direct effects. Whatever it is, the importance of tourism in Nepal compared to India is obvious from the fact that the assessed contribution of tourism to GDP is much higher (4 per cent as against 1.4 per cent).

Traditionally, the highest number of tourist arrival—about 45 per cent—has been from Asia and Europe accounts for about 30 per cent. The number of tourists from India is about 30 per cent. This does not include the substantial number of Indian tourists who travel by road. Indians are the single largest group of tourists to Nepal.

The recent trends in arrival of international tourists to Nepal are not satisfactory. They are also pointers to the direction of future strategy.

**Arrivals ('000)**

| | *1990* | *1995* | *1998* | *1999* | *2000* | *2001* |
|---|---|---|---|---|---|---|
| South Asia | 3,158 | 4,200 | 5,219 | 5,777 | 6,091(5.4%) | 5,707(–6.3%) |
| Nepal | 255 | 363 | 464 | 492 | 464(–5.7%) | 363(–21.8%) |

**Receipts**

| | | | | | | |
|---|---|---|---|---|---|---|
| South Asia | 2,029 | 3,469 | 4,270 | 4,564 | 4,094(7.5) | |
| Nepal | 64 | 117 | 153 | 168 | 167(–0.6) | |

**Source of Arrivals ('000)**

| | *1996* | *1997* | *1998* | *1999* | *2000* |
|---|---|---|---|---|---|
| North America | 30 | 36 | 43 | 46 | 49 |
| West Europe | 132 | 137 | 151 | 164 | 159 |
| Asia | 137 | 148 | 165 | 167 | 125 |
| (India) | (122) | (133) | (143) | (140) | (95) |

It is true that the decline in receipts has been less than the decline in arrivals. It is necessary to strengthen this trend. In 2001 after the effects of 9 /11, arrivals to South Asia declined by 6.3 per cent whereas the fall in arrivals to Nepal was almost 22 per cent. During this time Asia Pacific and SE Asia registered positive increase. Nepal's negative growth can be attributed to a lot of factors outside the area of tourism, but in a situation where the long haul destinations were discarded, Nepal had a golden opportunity of wooing the regional tourists. East Asia was the only region, which showed good increase during this period

In recent times the tourism profile of Nepal has shown a rather disturbing trend. The last 3 /4 years have been difficult for South Asia and Nepal had its share of problems. But even prior to that, while the number of arrivals was steadily growing, there was gradual decline in earnings. In 1994–95, for example, there was 11 per cent increase in arrivals but 32 per cent decline in receipts. That happens when the length of stay decreases or tourists spend less. In ecologically fragile tourism scenario of the country, three areas should merit attention to reverse this trend. The marketing strategy should focus on the quality of tourists. Internally, product development should concentrate on value addition. Existing products should be packaged in such a way that they hold interest of tourists for a longer period. More products should be developed at the same time and shopping and souvenirs should be part of the overall plans for product development.

The recent developments in international tourists arrivals to Nepal is not satisfactory and shows the directions in which future strategy should be focused.

**Arrivals ('000)**

| | *1990* | *1995* | *1998* | *1999* | *2000* | *2001* |
|---|---|---|---|---|---|---|
| South Asia | 3,158 | 4,200 | 5,219 | 5,777 | 6,091(5.4%) | 5,707(–6.3%) |
| Nepal | 255 | 363 | 464 | 492 | 464(–5.7%) | 363(–21.8%) |

**Receipts**

| | | | | | |
|---|---|---|---|---|---|
| South Asia | 2,029 | 3,469 | 4,270 | 4,564 | 4,094(7.5%) |
| Nepal | 64 | 117 | 153 | 168 | 167(–0.6%) |

**Source of Arrivals**

| | *1996* | *1997* | *1998* | *1999* | *2000* |
|---|---|---|---|---|---|
| North America | 30 | 36 | 43 | 46 | 49 |
| West Europe | 132 | 137 | 151 | 164 | 159 |
| Asia | 137 | 148 | 165 | 167 | 125 |
| (India) | (122) | (133) | (143) | (140) | (95) |

These illustrative figures show that happily the decline in receipts have been less than the decline in arrivals. It is necessary to strengthen this trend. In 2001, after the effects of 9/11 arrivals to South Asia fell by 6.3 per cent but Nepal registered the highest fall of almost 22 per cent. During this time Asia Pacific and SE Asia showed positive growth. Nepal's negative growth can be attributed to a lot of factors, which are outside the area of tourism. But it was a period when the long haul destinations were being avoided for shorter travels. Nepal had a golden opportunity of attracting a portion of the regional tourists. Thailand and Malaysia successfully launched a campaign to attract the high spending Indian tourists through a sustained marketing policy and reaped good dividends. This should have been an example both for India and Nepal. Unfortunately the tourists from India has shown drastic decline in recent times.

This is a time to think of long-term policy and Nepal is placed in an advantageous position because it has already put in place a forward looking organizational structure which can take on this responsibility. The Nepal Tourism Board is a very good example of public–private partnership. The Tourism Development Fund is also an innovative idea. The Tourism Advisory Council allows public participation in tourism development. India has only recently constituted the advisory council but Nepal has shown a lead in respect of the others.

Nepal and India can both benefit from a pragmatic cooperation in tourism. Such cooperation should be based on complementing the comparative advantage of each in which each country sees tangible benefits. India has the advantage of a growing long and medium haul outbound passengers, which is growing faster than the inbound. They are also considered to be very high spenders. The outbound from India is assessed to be around 4 million. In addition, the domestic tourist is booming and has reached 230 million. A substantial part of these tourists are potential tourists to Nepal because of geographical proximity and religious affinity. Two of the major religions of the world—Hinduism and Buddhism—and the enchanting Himalayan ranges are among the most valuable assets shared by the two countries on which a very robust tourism cooperation policy could be built.

Nepal has tourism potential that specially suit the modern tourist's psyche. The new tourism is eco-friendly and the ecologically fragile mountain region of Nepal can attract a lot of tourists on its eco-tourism policy alone. More and more travellers are now looking for new and unique experience in travel and Nepal and India can provide such uniqueness. Nepal is synonymous with adventure and Indian products can supplement the attractions of such adventure.

One of the fall out of the 9/11 events has been greater attention to regional tourism. 9/11 changed the structure and content of travel and tourism business. In this new scenario short haul travel has been more favoured. Outbound tourist from the Asia pacific and the SE Asian region has registered highest growth and in fact China is projected to top the list of outbound tourists by 2020. One important feature of the outbound tourists from this region a very large number of them travel for partly religious purposes. Buddhism is a common thread of all these countries. But interest in Buddhism is no longer confined to Buddhists alone. When the whole world was reeling under the effects of 9/11, the SE Asia region registered growth of 12 per cent Nepal and India, with such strong advantage in religious tourism failed to take advantage of this phenomenon.

Product change and product diversification are urgently required in Nepal to give Nepal tourism a fresh image. Many of its most used products, be if the lovely mountains or the veneered temple of Lord Pashupati, are showing signs of fatigue. This is an area where joint collaboration is possible. India has many bad examples of managing religious places; it also has some very fine examples of managing very large establishments like the Vaishno Devi and the temple of Lord Tirupati. The expertise available could be shared for common benefit as a better-managed and maintained Pashupati temple itself may see a large influx of Indian tourists to Nepal. India recently has shown a new trend in public-private partnership by allowing the private sector to maintain important monuments—an example which can be shared by Nepal as well.

Buddhism is a great tourism attraction today but Nepal—the birth place of Buddha—and India—the place where Lord Buddha attained enlightenment—have not jointly or individually, adequately promoted or marketed it. The Buddhist circuit in India and Nepal should be developed as one complementary circuit. Similarly, the Himalayas, which are used mostly for high range mountaineering in Nepal and trekking in India, could be promoted as complementary adventure tourism products.

There are immense potential for tourism cooperation between the two countries in which both can derive economic benefits. Any such cooperation to be meaningful some areas for action can be identified.

1. *Institutional Framework*—At present there is no organizational set up for continuous interaction on tourism. It is necessary to create a permanent platform for interaction among government, private sector, regional and international organizations like PATA, WTO etc. Presently, the arrangements are purely ad hoc and temporary.
2. *Joint Marketing*—Ideologically, it is a right step; conceptually it is sound. But it does not happen in practice because tourism development is seen as

competitive and not complementary. Joint marketing will succeed only if it is based on a concept of mutual benefit. Both the countries should develop complementary circuits, which can be marketed as one new product.

3. *Connectivity*—Joint marketing will remain an idea only until the product can be jointly shared. Combined connectivity is an essential part of such cooperation. Viable collaboration between Nepal and India involving the national carriers-domestic and international—can link the Buddhist circuits. The present link of Guwahati with Bangkok can be enhanced by linking Bhutan and Kathmandu and also having Bodh Gaya as a feeder.
4. *Human Resource Development*—HRD is seen as one of the five most important influences on tourism growth in the future. Tourism is a service industry, but it is no longer confined to providing a service only. The totality of service provided should create a unique experience for the tourist. HRD in tourism should therefore develop a total manager concept. On the other hand technological revolution, particularly in IT has changed the tourism and travel business. Technology is all comprehensive and fast changing. Present day managers are therefore required to be on a continuous training mode if they are not to become outdated. Globalisation and greater labour mobility makes it necessary to have more harmonization of training materials and contents across borders. The net effect of all these developments is that training has become a crucial component of tourism strategy and training has become a very expensive input. Government therefore feel that the HRD issues should be primarily be looked after by the industry. Industry, on the other hand, being fragmented and composed of many small players, is unable to take any initiative.

For the development of tourism human resource development should find the place of priority in Nepal. Unfortunately, because of the constraints mentioned this area might tend to suffer. Fortunately, India has a very elaborate network of tourism education and training involving both the public and private sector. To save on the overheads the infrastructure available with India can be shared.

5. Similarly, India has very strong entrepreneurial capability in hotel and other hospitality sector infrastructure. Collaboration to improve the quality of present infrastructure and to look at new areas is possible. One such new area is convention tourism. There are many examples of two countries jointly hosting international conferences. The last General Assembly of the World Tourism Organisation was jointly hosted by Korea and Japan. Joint collaboration in this area would improve the attraction of any proposal to host such a conference.

There are a few important issues, which must always be kept in view while taking a long-term policy perspective on tourism. The first is the need for internal coordination. Tourism does not happen in isolation. It requires an integrated approach. Other components of tourism like environment, culture, internal security, communication etc. play a very important in fashioning the total tourism product should be properly coordinated.

Image of a country is sometimes a problem. Nepal has suffered on this count recently, so has India to some extent. Sometimes media creates the image and often it is not deserved. But the fact is that Nepal now does not enjoy the image of a peaceful heaven on earth that it had earlier. But things change and public memory is often short. It should be sound policy nevertheless, to acknowledge the reality, as it is today and to work together to remove it as soon as possible.

To some extent the old magic can be revived by people's participation in a large scale in tourism regeneration of Nepal. People should participate not only in the development of the product but also in sharing the benefits.

At the core of tourism policy should be the primary concern for sustainable tourism. For every country, sustainable development is the compulsive requirement. For Nepal, where nature is the most valuable asset, it is more so. In fact people's participation is the other side of sustainable tourism. In both the countries, local Agenda 21 for travel and tourism should be another area of strong collaboration.

As can be seen, one disquieting feature of Nepal tourism has been fall in arrivals from India. Some positive action needs to be taken to correct this trend. First should be more people to people and organization-to-organization contact to remove undue sensitivity. For this reason the existence of an organizational set up for continuous interaction on tourism would be very beneficial. As Mahatma Gandhi said, "travel is the language of peace." More tourism between the two countries would not only help Nepal, it would also facilitate other issues in bilateral relationship.

To encourage more of Indian tourists Nepal tourism must have much more visible presence in India. Continuous marketing by Malaysia and Thailand have created a stronger urge among the Indians to visit these places. Nepal's attractions should be marketed in a similar manner.

It is necessary to facilitate road journeys to Nepal as an alternative. In the bilateral issues, the quality of roads leading to and from Nepal should feature. In fact some of the most suitable areas of collaboration could be construction of highways linking the Buddhist sites, wayside amenities of international standards, tourists coaches of quality etc.

In the past, for most upper middle class Indian tourists Nepal was the ultimate destination in two respects—shopping and honeymoon. The shopping urge has diminished with liberalization in India and availability of foreign goods more freely locally. Yet, even now Dubai and Malaysia attract a lot of tourists for shopping alone. There is no reason why an imaginative marketing and economic policy could not build Nepal as another Dubai nearer home.

And, Nepal can still be a paradise for honeymooners if the everlasting beauty of the mountains, the snows, the meadows, the rivers and the charm of the colourful people could be offered in an atmosphere of idyllic bliss. It is all possible and can be done. It can be done better and quicker if we join hands. It should start with a campaign to create awareness about the immense contribution of tourism to socio-economic development of both the countries. The world is very competitive. It will be a pity if we lose out on our god gifted assets by failing to take action in time.

# *PART IV*

# MISCELLANEOUS

# 13

# Tourism: The Worst of Times, The Best of Times*

International tourism is now passing through one of the worst periods. After the 9/11 events, termed by the world Tourism Organisation as 'the deepest crisis in tourism history', it was slowly clawing back to the growth path with a slightly lower than projected growth of 3.1 per cent by the end of 2002. But the New Year started with war clouds in the horizon, oil and gold prices rose alarmingly and many stock exchanges dropped. Tourism, highly price sensitive, faced another uncertain period with fears of slower economic recovery.

But in India, already reeling under the adverse impact of a series of events like the international sanction after the nuclear explosion, the Kargil war, earthquake and law and order problems in Gujarat, terrorist attack in the Parliament, and badly mauled by a 24 per cent decline after the 9/11 events, the latest budget gives a lot to cheer about. The budget, for the first time, takes a long-term perspective of the fundamentals of tourism.

A common lament in the tourism industry used to be that 'tourism is what everyone talks about and no one cares'. In every conference, the doyens of the industry would discuss how neglected the industry was—a view strongly in consonance with the feelings in the Ministry of Tourism—that not a single

* Published in *Hindustan Times,* April 3, 2003 under caption—"Destination India" in the Edit Page.

word was uttered by successive Finance Ministers in the budget speeches about tourism. In 1998, the World Travel and Tourism Council made an assessment of the economic impact of tourism in India. It was very enthusiastic in its forecast and projected that by 2010 travel and tourism 'economy' could provide, among others, 8 million new jobs and contribute Rs. 5,00,000 crore to GDP 'if' a few pragmatic policies were followed. On top of the agenda was, 'an integrated strategy' and 'strong, sustained policy implementation driven from the top'. Hoping for a new dawn in tourism in the new millennium, the Ministry of Tourism, rightly pursued in the last few years a single agenda of creating wider awareness about the importance of tourism and launched a well-noticed publicity campaign 'tourism touches everyone'.

All that seems to have paid dividends now. The first ray of sun of the new millennium in the Andaman and Nicobar islands seems to have ushered in a new vision on tourism. In his first Independence Day message of the millennium from the ramparts of the historic Red Fort, the Prime Minister spoke about the importance of tourism. In the budget speech that followed the Finance Minister clearly echoed the new found trust in tourism and announced "tourism constitutes a priority area".

The tourism industry, particularly the hotel sector will no doubt be jubilant about the direct concessions announced in the latest budget. The travel agents and the tour operators will perhaps continue to grumble that their concern for the service tax was not addressed. However, the most significant part of the budget for tourism is not the concessions but the recognition of the multi-dimensional nature of tourism and the importance of intersectoral linkages for its promotion—a strain that keeps coming up in the entire speech.

It is clear in the FM's approach to infrastructure development. Improvements in roads, rails, airports and sea-ports—what else the tourism sector can ask for? The quality of airport infrastructure in India has long been cited as a major bottleneck for tourism. The phenomenal boom in international tourism between 1960 and 2000, from barely 70 m arrivals to 700 m was largely pushed by the developments in civil aviation. In the coming years too, improvements in civil aviation technology will be a major influence in the growth of tourism. The technology of flying is changing fast; so is the airframe manufacturing technology. And despite the body blow to civil aviation industry after the 9/11 events, the volume of passenger traffic is expected to increase tremendously. In 1997, the scheduled air traffic was around 1,500 billion revenue passenger miles, which is projected to almost double by 2005 and become 4,000 billion RPMs by 2015. India's airport infrastructure is not capable of handling any big growth in traffic. Not one airport is designed, it is reported, to handle the bigger more efficient new age aircraft. At the beginning of this century, India had 120 airports, and another 329 airstrips as against 76 in China. Only 13 of the airports were in profit and the top five handled 73.5 per cent of the traffic. Less than two per cent domestic tourists travelled by air. In this sector there is much that needs to be done. The happy thing is that a beginning is being made.

Successive exit surveys have shown that the foreign tourists find internal travel by road and rail to be cumbersome, inconvenient and insufficient. The Ministry of Tourism had drafted an action plan for comprehensive and integrated development of tourism related rail, road and air facilities of international standard for which the resource requirement was around Rs 45,000 crore. As resource of such magnitude was nowhere in sight the action plan was quickly forgotten. The FM, by providing Rs 6,000 crore in one year through innovative funding mechanisms has revived great hopes of positive action in this area.

One major problem of marketing India abroad has been the image of the country as a high cost destination. High cost of hotel accommodation has been part of that image. Within that, the multiplicity of taxes account for anything between 20 to 35 per cent of the hotel bill. The bold step of abolishing the expenditure tax, strongly argued for by the Tourism Ministry all these years, in one stroke makes the hotels 10 per cent cheaper. The abolition of service tax may reduce it by another 5 to 8 per cent. The entire tourism industry will now pray that the FM's expectation and recommendation to the states to abolish the luxury tax will be listened to. However, most of the resource starved states still consider tourism to be an eminently taxable elitist sector and may not see the income and employment-generating impact of tourism as the FM does. It will need all the persuasive skill of the Ministry of Tourism and sustained campaigning by the industry to convince the states that a lowering of taxes may in fact bring in more revenue through higher turnover as was shown by the experience of Goa.

Convention tourism is big business in the world today and India has missed out on really big convention tourism for lack of convention centers of international standard. Quite often proposals have remained at the drawing board stage because the heavy investment required makes the project weak in viability. Government too, had avoided it on the plea that it was a commercial activity to be handled by the private sector only. The proposal to bridge the viability gap through an innovative funding scheme is a very definite step for public private partnership. A lot remains to be done though, to get suitable incentives on land policy, to cut the maze of 38 odd approvals required to put up such a project and to coordinate it with other components of a convention center like supporting hotel and transport linkages. But the ball clearly is the court of India Inc. now.

The most refreshing and optimistic feature for tourism in the budget is the strain of strong inter-sectoral linkages that the FM establishes. It shows in his approach to infrastructure; it is implicit in his health planning—projecting India as a health destination; it is apparent in re-introducing the LTC. And to top it all the India Development Initiative to promote India would be the ideal plank to launch the Incredible India brand. The industry would perhaps dearly wish the FM did something to tackle the problem of very high cost of internal air travel. But then, the budget cannot be a catalogue for each ministry's action agenda.

# 14

# Back on the Road*

Two days after the tsunami of December 26, newspapers carried photographs of tourists back on the beaches of Phuket—one of the locations worst hit. In February, Phuket will host the executive council meeting of the World Tourism Organisation, the UN's specialised agency on tourism.

Such acts are symbolic of the spirit of tourism. The roving, wandering urge of human beings is not to be thwarted by nature's fury. Tourism is a resilient industry. It bounces back after every crisis. In the year after the Gulf War of 1991, world tourism experienced an unprecedented eight per cent growth.

Even so, the first four years of the new millennium have been traumatic for the Asia Pacific region. In 2003, an unknown virus called SARS did more damage than any terrorist attacks. Asia Pacific tourism lost 12 million arrivals—four times the number of tourists India sees in one year. But, as expected, in 2004 Asia Pacific arrivals hit the 300 million mark. The region is well on its way to becoming the world's most visited destination by 2020. Notwithstanding the tsunami disaster, there is no doubt tourism will bounce back, perhaps as early as 2005.

Indeed, a significant number of the tsunami-affected people would wish so. Let's not underestimate the economic power of tourism. There are reports from Sri Lanka that in the worst

* Published in *Hindustan Times*, January 21, 2005.

affected areas people are keener on long-term rehabilitation through quick restoration of tourism, rather than limping to normality through relief doles.

Given quick assessments, only about 10 per cent of the tourist attractions in the Andaman Sea coasts and islands have been damaged. Seventy per cent of Sri Lanka's tourism infrastructure too is reported safe. Sri Lanka still hopes to reach its target of 6,00,000 tourists this year. Thailand prepares to get back to normal by March, even though the Phuket region, which generates about $3 billion in tourism earnings annually, was badly hit.

The pain and trauma of the tragedy apart, there could be some opportunities and lessons for India. Like the fear of flying a few years ago—immediately after 9/11—the fear of the angry seas will influence decisions by tourists. Holiday-makers trying to run away from the cold, grey skies of a European or American winter must seek alternatives to the beaches of Thailand, Sri Lanka or the Maldives.

In the past fortnight, the Indian tourism minister appropriately perceived this opportunity and advocated "visas on arrival" for tourists who may have had to change their plans at the last minute. Unfortunately not much has been heard about this initiative. If implemented it would have demonstrated that the much talked about "visa on arrival" scheme is, after all, not such a difficult thing to operate. It could be a regular feature, not limited to emergency situations and disaster years.

In any case, even if such moves do attract more tourists, we still have to address larger internal problems. Even before the tsunami, hotels in all our metros were packed. Goa, our flagship beach destination, had no rooms available. The travel industry has been crying hoarse for adequate hotel infrastructure but how that becomes possible is a million dollar question.

Entrepreneurs complain of absence of a pragmatic land

policy; 38 approvals are required to set up a hotel. Delhi's master plan had earmarked hotel sites in all major localities. They have vanished into history. The "Incredible India" campaign helped bring tourists, but infrastructure growth remains an issue.

At the beginning of the millennium, India's shortage was estimated at 30,000 rooms. This figure is not static. Today the requirement would be much larger, given the 25 per cent growth rate in tourist arrivals. Take Goa. As on April 1, 2003, according to Tourism Ministry figures, it had only 5,832 hotel rooms, taking in all categories from "unclassified" to "five star".

There is a growing mismatch between demand and supply. While hoteliers are happy in the short run—their rooms are full—tourism in the larger sense is the long-term casualty. This leads to distortions. The travel industry has told the tourism minister of instances of unethical practices by some hoteliers, who refuse to honour old bookings and ask for higher rates. Successfully wooing tourists without corresponding rooms and facilities is an obvious anomaly. It ends up creating the impression that India is a high cost destination.

The saturation of Goa should also invite attention. It is a pity that a country with such a long coastline can't offer world-class alternatives to Goa. Global competition is stiff. Prospective tourists turned away due to lack of accommodation will not persist with India. They will establish a relationship with easier and cheaper options.

It is time now to launch a marketing strategy to promote other exotic beach locations—in Kerala, Orissa, Maharashtra for instance. In the Ninth and Tenth Five Year Plans, the government had mooted, adopting the model of Cancun in Mexico, the idea of Special Tourism Area (STA) development. This called for comprehensive infrastructure development in chosen destinations, in partnership with the private sector. The Maharashtra government had gone one step further. It had declared Sindhudurg, adjoining Goa, as a "Tourism District". Some progress was also made in Bekal, Kerala.

But the fact is these places are still far from being considered alternatives to Goa. The STA idea has not quite taken off. Initially there were misgivings in Goa about Sindhudurg. It was felt that the two would end up competing for the same small pie.

Such a narrow view makes no sense in a big country like India. Globally tourism is booming and there are opportunities for all. The unique Puri and Chandipur beaches in Orissa, Daman and Diu, and Tamil Nadu's (Mamallapuram)—destinations selected as part of the STA strategy—could be linked in a grand circuit to supplement Goa. India has unique destinations and the Incredible India campaign has brought them to the world's view. We need to seize the moment, create an experience for tourists that matches our ad lines.."

# 15

# India: Looking Ahead*

For India, the PATA conference could not have come at a more opportune time. The effects of the events of September 11, subsequent Afghanistan war, the terrorist attack on the Parliament, the citadel of Indian democracy, — all these dealt a severe blow to the recent efforts to promote tourism as an input in national economic development plans. The tourism industry needs the helping hand and encouragement of the international fraternity to come out of this gloom. On the other hand this was also a period when the government had shown greater awareness about the importance of tourism than was seen for a long time. The Prime Minister had chosen the occasion of the Independence Day to send the important message to the country that tourism was a vital ingredient of the nation's development efforts. And sweeping aside the constant criticism of the industry that tourism was not getting its due recognition in the national planning, the Finance Minister announced —"tourism constitutes a priority area". In the backdrop of serious discussions on future global concerns, if the conference could help the Indian tourism industry to build long term marketing networks, and could strongly endorse the government's recent initiatives, and lend PATA's support in whatever way it can, to further those objectives, the conference would have been worth-while.

---

* Published in "Trav Talk" in the Oceasion of PATA Annual Conference in New Delhi April 2002.

India and PATA have been together for a long time and India's problems are not unknown to its members. However, most delegates would be wondering, why international tourists arrival to India remains so low inspite of India's great attractions. Between 1980 and 1997, when the biggest tourism boom took place, India's average annual growth rate was comparable to the world average. But that is a poor consolation considering that China's growth rate has been almost three times that of India, Indonesia's 3.5 times, and Thailand's more than double. Saying that India lacks infrastructure, as is commonly said, is too generic and simplistic an explanation. There are numerous small things to be done by all concerned to bring up India's position in the global scenario. But the big things that various organisations like the WTO, the WITC and PATA have been suggesting boils down to a few. First, tourism should be provided national priority. It is required not to satisfy the ego of the industry about a status, but primarily to emphasise the fact that tourism infrastructure can not be built in isolation. Tourism is a complex multi-disciplinary activity which defies simple definition. All the vital components can work in co-ordination only when there is a national understanding. Second, all the activities can not be handled by the government alone. Partnership with the private sector, the NGOs and other stake holders is is the key of modern tourism development strategy. Government have to create that atmosphere where the private initiative flourishes and is not sapped. Third, for such partnership to grow, a regime of liberalised economic policy is essential. The financial and monetary policies must be conducive to the growth of the tourism sector. The present atmosphere with multiplicity and high incidence of taxes is widely perceived to be not development friendly. In the highly competitive world of today, India, being branded as 'high cost' destination is losing the advantage. And fourth, in this service industry, HRD must be at the top of the agenda for action, both for the government as well for the industry. One question that will be widely asked is, what can PATA do for India? Though

PATA does not take up country specific programmes as such, it can certainly help the Indian tourism industry in a number of ways. The tourism sector does not really have a strong lobby for creating public opinion and in helping formulation of public policy. PATA with its enormous reputation worldwide, could help in formation of such a platform. PATA's greatest strength has been India's weakest—marketing. It could certainly help in building up India's marketing network. If the government of India is so willing, PATA could help in formulation of a long term marketing strategy and help in putting it in place. Similarly, the complexity of the training requirements of the future and the resultant high cost have put HRD in the backstage at a time when it is needed most. To overcome cost, networking of training institutions and harmonisation of course contents are needed. To achieve the highest spread of tourism education, PATA had started way back in 1970s a programme of 'training of trainers'. India could very greatly benefit from such schemes.

From the beginning PATA was proud of its philosophy of "working to make this world a better place to be." PATA had helped in the awareness campaign in India. Today, the industry has to provide the leadership in firmly putting in place ethical and sustainable standards. India should feel proud and happy having hosted the conference if it creates an atmosphere to enthuse the larger tourism community to start a movement for sustainable tourism concepts in India as PATA has been trying globally.

# 16

# PATA's Vision

My association with PATA has not been long, but it has been very pleasant and rewarding. It has been very aptly said that PATA is not only the story of great events and achievements, it is also the coming together of some outstanding persons. As the chairman of the golden jubilee year conference at Kualalumpur in 2001,it was my privilege to interact with some of these doyens of the travel and tourism industry, remarkable persons in their respective fields, always brimming with enthusiasm about doing something new. Many of them, life members, still continue the early threads of the organisation and regale you with delightful anecdotes of the glorious journey.

It is a story of a vision—started with two, now spreading to twenty two thousand. The vision has been changing over the years—initially it was marketing, in the post war economic scenario it was concern for economic development—but PATA has been always characterised by its collective desire and capability to look ahead. The strength of an organisation depends on its capacity to reflect the members' interests. PATA was started with the objective of marketing the beautiful pacific region and therefore marketing remains at the core of its concerns. And PATA has been doing it admirably, certainly making its contribution in making this region the fastest growing area in tourism. Early in the 90s PATA had started looking at 2000 and beyond. Its vision document 'Direction

* Written on occasion of PATA Annual Conference in New Delhi in April 2000.

2000' set the objective clearly — to become the leader of, and authority on, Pacific Asia travel.

It is significant that in the 50th year conference PATA talked about "proud past and promising future". Naturally 50 proud years was a cause for celebrations. The theme for the New Delhi conference is "Tourism — Looking Ahead and Beyond". In the post-9/11 scenario nothing could be more pertinent. In Kualalumpur we had talked about the future. I had said in my speech that, the primary challenge before PATA was its ability to be in tune with the spirit of change. In Hongkong and Kualalumpur we were trying to put our heads together to find ways to expand the PATA family network and to put PATA — PATA Chapter relationship on a solid foundation on shared ideology and commitment. "A vibrant dynamic relationship of this wider family" I said," based on the pride of belonging and the privilege of sharing should be our launching pad for the 21st century initiatives." We were looking at the complex issue or PATA's geographical boundaries. When the industry is global, and enthusiasm of members is universal, many thought, geographical boundaries for doing good is unreal. In all these years, in the midst of hard struggle, PATA has not wavered from the idealism of making this world a better place to be through tourism.

Now in New Delhi in the midst of the gloomy travel and tourism sçenario, as the industry picks up the threads of the recovery process, PATA's leadership role will again be put to test. There could not be a better challenge to begin the second part of the 'Century' journey and no better ambience than the backdrop of the wonder that is India, where the air breathes the wisdom of thousand of years of culture and civilisation.

# 17

# India Welcomes PATA*

It has been almost quarter of a century since India had the privilege of hosting a PATA annual conference. This has also been a period of tremendous changes in the travel and tourism scenario. Heralded by rapid advances in the civil aviation technology, great changes in the world geo-political situations and the vastly improved safety perception about travel and a rapid growth in the world economy, tourism entered the new millennium as the largest industry in the world. And in this remarkable journey, PATA had a very glorious role to play.

In Kuala Lumpur last year, PATA celebrated its 50 years on the theme of "proud past and promising future". The New Delhi conference is, in all essence, a continuation of the same celebrations. When PATA was celebrating its 40th year, the legendary James A. Michener, who, perhaps more than anyone else, brought a romantic image of the Pacific to the rest of the world, wrote that PATA had "accomplished more than any other travel organisation in educating and marketing Pacific travel, as well as maintaining and improving Pacific tourist destinations -environmentally, socially and culturally." The theme of the New Delhi conference, very appropriately is, "looking ahead and beyond." Looking ahead everyone does, often guided by past experiences. But looking beyond

* Written on the Occasion of the PATA Annual Conference at New Delhi, April 2002.

requires a vision. PATA was borne out of such a vision and continue to be guided by a long-term perspective. Originally its primary objective was to market the "beautiful pacific." In the region touched by the pacific which has 75 per cent of the world's population, marketing of tourism as a means of improving the lot of the people has been at the core of all PATA activities and in fact has been it's forte. It may be pertinent to remind the delegates that in this land of ours, one of the five dreams of the great philosopher Aurobindo was "for the resurgence and liberation of the peoples of Asia and her return to a great role in the progress of human civilisation."

From the very beginning, concern for a qualitative long term approach to tourism and a desire to use the resources and expertise to make the world a better place to be, has inspired the activities of PATA. In the very first conference, Earl Warren had reminded the delegates that the objective of all growth was peace -"first, last and always."

Mahatma Gandhi had beautifully summed up this role of tourism when he described travel as the language of peace.

These expressions may guide the deliberations in the New Delhi conference taking place against the backdrop of one of the worst crises the travel and tourism industry is facing. Happily, all the present assessments show that the industry will soon rally back to its projected growth path. But a long- term strategy rather than panic reaction to cope with such emergencies will have to be evolved. The industry must also put its heads together to find solutions to the more worrying fact of world economic recession continuing longer than anticipated. As the tourism component of individual consumption is more elastic to income changes, attempts to win back the confidence in flying may not be a complete solution. Still PATA can provide the leadership to develop new alignments and new marketing strategies based on co-operation rather than competition alone, if the region as a whole is to benefit from the umbrella support of the organisation. Beyond the glittering social and cultural events and bon-homie of the 'who is who' of the world's travel and tourism industry, each PATA conference is a landmark in the journey of vision and in tackling the challenges that confront the industry. More than any other conference in the recent past, the New Delhi conference is taking place at a time when the travel and tourism industry is facing daunting challenges. Everywhere the government and the industry together are trying to find solutions to falling tourists arrivals, large job cuts and resultant effects in the economy. PATA was the first organisation to recognise the importance of public-private partnership and in fact was founded on that concept of collaboration. India, starting late in the liberalisation process, finds that it has a long way to go in developing a meaningful partnership. Therefore the conference can serve the purpose of awareness creation in India on some of the vital issues. It can galvanise India's latest awakening in the tourism sector to start a new chapter of progress. The beleaguered travel and tourism industry will also be looking forward to concrete action programmes to rebuild the industry. The New Delhi conference, we hope, will be a landmark of bold initiatives on all the future challenges as PATA starts its second part of the century journey.

# 18

# PATA: Looking to the Future*

"If You Do not Change, You Can Become Extinct."

—*Dr. Spencer Johnson,*

(Who Moved My Cheese)

When PATA started 50 years back, it was motivated primarily by the interest of its members to market the "beautiful pacific". Things have changed since. Shrinking time and space, disappearing barriers of borders have given shape to that soaring, roving liberal human spirit. But as it is said, the future is not what it used to be. The world geo-political configurations are changing beyond recognition. Consumer behaviour are fast changing. And there are incredible developments in technology, changing at ever accelerating speed, encompassing all spheres of human activities as never before. PATA has to constantly look at its future options to be in tune with time if it has to maintain its predominant position in the travel and tourism industry.

At the time of its 40th year celebrations PATA had looked at the future—its 'Direction 2000' was a bold document of vision and ideas. It talked about a global orientation, it raised issues of environment and education as future concerns, and still broadly desired to pursue qualitative long-term approach to tourism. Even at that time there were serious doubts and debates about going beyond the primary concern of marketing and the members' collective interest. There were strong feelings

* Published in Trav Talk. April 2002.

against going beyond the primary objective of enhancing the business of its members.

If PATA is to be true to its avowed desire of making "the world a better place to be", and if it is to be alive "environmentally, socially and culturally" as Michener had said, it must seriously tackle these issues. It cannot be immune to the fact that increasing inequality co-exists with growing prosperity of the world. In my address as the Chairman of the Kualalumpur conference, I had drawn attention to the fact that during the period that tourism arrivals in the world doubled, sixty countries of the world were getting steadily poorer than before.

In its Direction 2000, PATA talked about evolving a philosophy that is global in its sweep. In its future role of leadership it must evolve strategies to help empower the developing nations to access emerging technologies which will be the most crucial influence on tourism development in the future. It must focus on Human Resource Development that can help the developing nations to acquire the expertise to provide quality services. In the future "experience economy" where the consumer will be the 'king' the competitive edge will be provided by the quality of the human resources. PATA must have a significant and visible role in enthusing its members to adopt training and education as part of their existence. It must help evolve harmonised course contents, make available the benefits of research and technology to all through networking and must lead a movement to spread the tourism education to reach large areas now uncovered.

PATA must be alive to the compulsive need of putting the practice of sustainable tourism firmly in place. There are daunting challenges of adjusting the needs of tourism development to the compulsions of environmental preservation, of putting ethics and human rights at the core of its concern.

PATA has a big role to play in the future. To be alive and growing, it must look at change as constant. It is fortunate that it has the capacity to change and make a difference.

# 19

# Regional Cooperation in Tourism*

It is an honour for me to participate in this important event. First of all, I would like to express, on behalf of my Secretary-General, his most sincere regrets at not being able to join you today due to his prior firm commitments. However, he has asked me to convey to you his best wishes for a successful meeting. WTO has very active over the last few months in promoting the recovery of the Asian tourism industry after the devastating impacts of SARS and we fully support initiatives such as this meeting.

We were all extremely pleased when, on the 5th of July, the World Health Organization (WHO) confirmed that no new cases have been reported around the world since 15 June and that the SARS epidemic has been brought under control. WHO's SARS travel warnings have been lifted in all of the affected countries. The tourism industry had anxiously awaited this good news because the past 22 months have been a period of unprecedented problems.

WTO would like to also commend all those authorities and individuals who contributed to the victory against SARS — a special mention should be made to doctors, nurses and all other medical staff. In their fight for their community, they also contributed to preserving the tourism industry worldwide from a larger disaster. It is due to their dedication

*Statement made by Mr. M.P. Bezbaruah, WTO Permanent Representative, on behalf of WTO, at the Special Meeting of Tourism Ministers of ASEAN, China, Japan and Korea Beijing, China, 09 August 2003.

and courage that a recovery is now possible, for China, for Asia and for the rest of the world.

* * *

SARS is just the latest crisis in a string of troubles that began with the tragic September 11th attacks on the United States -troubles that caused the first dip in international tourism since we started keeping track fifty years ago.

The recovery from September 11th has been slow, not only because of the shocking nature of those attacks, but because of sluggish economies in Germany, Japan and the United States -the world's main tourist generating markets.

But just as the tourism sector began to recuperate last year, there were new terrorist attacks — in Djerba, in Mombassa, in Bali and in Casablanca among other places. Uncertainty over where terrorists might strike next caused tourists to stick to familiar destinations or stay close to home.

At the same time, uncertainty about the outbreak of war in Iraq depressed tourism activity even more, as people postponed their travel plans waiting to see what would happen in the Middle East.

Then just as the conflict in Iraq was ending and the horizon began to clear, a new and entirely unforeseen crisis emerged. SARS has had a devastating and wholly unexpected impact on tourism in the Asia-Pacific region -way beyond the impact of the war in Iraq. Repercussions have been felt throughout the world and WTO has identified three main reasons for this:

- SARS appeared from the very beginning as an unknown and unpredictable disease. The World Health Organization reported that it never experienced a phenomenon like this in its history. It was also the first time in its history that WHO issued travel warnings. Some of them may have seemed to be overly severe, but we have to take into consideration that disease reappeared in Toronto just as the city was about to start a big campaign to re-launch its tourism -proving how little we still know about SARS.

- Secondly, East Asia and the Pacific -which posted an 8.3 per cent growth rate in tourist arrivals last year - has proven to be the driving force of growth for international tourism. The SARS epidemic came after the sinister attack in Bali, which was the worst in the history of world tourism since the Second World War and had a tremendous impact on the region. Even though SARS mainly affected this region, its ripple effect was felt worldwide.
- Thirdly, the SARS epidemic is perceived by the public to be intrinsically linked to tourism. It's true that the disease was spread by people who traveled from one country to another and that one of the early outbreaks occurred in a hotel, but transmission has taken place essentially among household or hospital contacts with little or no evidence of it being passed among strangers engaging in ordinary tourism.

Ladies and gentlemen,

It's no secret that tourism is an extremely sensitive industry. It's vulnerable to war, to terrorism, to economic problems, to natural disasters and to disease. But at the same time, it is a very resilient industry.

The habit of taking holidays and business trips is so ingrained that people may delay their departures or change their destination but they will still continue to travel. This is why -in spite of all the obstacles- international arrivals grew by more than 3 per cent last year.

Tourism has demonstrated time after time its ability to bounce back after a crisis. It proved this ability following the first Gulf War in 1991 and it showed tremendous resiliency once again following the Asian Economic Crisis in 1997 and 98. That is why -despite all the obstacles- we remain optimistic about the long-term health of the industry. That is also why

WTO has not adjusted its long-term growth forecast. We still foresee international tourist arrivals hitting one billion by the year 2010 and we still predict that, on average, international tourism will grow by 4 per cent a year up until 2020.

No doubt, the SARS epidemic added a new element of uncertainty that clouded the immediate future and complicated recovery, especially in this part of the world.

Even so, recovery remains a certainty. Based on our observation of past crises, the SARS epidemic will only delay recovery -but maybe not by more than a few months. The economy is picking up again, especially in China, and people who postponed business meetings and vacations during the epidemic are now beginning to reschedule their trips.

We predict that the expected improvement in the global economic situation in the United States and Europe in the third quarter should lead to a notable increase in bookings and departures by the end of this year -an increase above and beyond the general increase in economic activity due to a pent-up demand for travel in recent months.

* * *

Of course recovery will not take place evenly around the world. Destinations that recover the fastest will be ones that work the most effectively during this critical recovery period which is why this Meeting comes at such an opportune moment.

Crisis Management is an issue that WTO has been dealing with since September 11 through the work of our Tourism Recovery Committee. The Committee includes tourism ministers and public officers and high-level representatives of the private sector. Members met to exchange ideas on how to reactivate the industry, ideas that have facilitated many good decisions by member countries on how to handle the difficult situation we've faced for the past two years.

To summarize this work and assist members with the recovery, WTO has prepared a booklet called "Crisis Guidelines for the Tourism Sector". We have focused on the topic of crisis management and presented the guidelines to members of the WTO Regional Commission for South Asia at its meeting in Nepal in May, as well as to the Regional Commission for East Asia and the Pacific at its meetings last month in Manila. We will also present them in September to our Middle East Regional Commission in Bahrein and we will hold a special session of the Recovery Committee within the framework of our General Assembly next October.

Three main lessons have emerged from our work in the area of crisis management.

First is the need for pre-crisis planning. The only way that you have a chance of managing a crisis successfully is by being prepared. By working on relationships ahead of time: relationships with the media, with police and all the other security agencies; by having properly trained staff ahead of time; and, by having enough working equipment in place to handle high-speed communications during a crisis.

The second lesson is the need for honest and transparent communication. The main objective of crisis management is to protect and rebuild the reputation of the destination and that's why it's fundamental to play the card of transparency. Whether you face a problem of terrorism or a major epidemic, being honest and transparent is essential because it strengthens the credibility on which your reputation is based.

During a crisis and afterwards, one of the best things to tell journalists and tour operators is: "Come and see for yourselves. Don't even let me influence you. Make your own judgment and report what you have seen." This is the best way to avoid distortion of the information.

The third lesson is the need for partnership and cooperation in dealing with a crisis and recovering from one. Partnerships need to be built on all levels: within government, with the private sector, with safety and security officials, with the media -and between different countries. At our level, this is what we are doing within our Recovery Committee.

It is actually during difficult times like these that cooperation within an organization such as WTO becomes more necessary and relevant than ever.

* * *

Ladies and gentlemen,

I'm certain that strategies for recovering from the SARS crisis are currently uppermost in your business plans and I can assure you that the World Tourism Organization has also been paying close attention to the evolution of this crisis. In June, at the height of the SARS epidemic, our Executive Council met to decide what to do about our General Assembly, which was set to begin on October 19th in Beijing. While it was impossible to make a decision in June, we have been holding consultations with the Chinese government since then. On 15 July 2003, at the WTO/Boao Forum for Asia Conference on Revitalising Asian Tourism, the WTO Secretary-General officially announced that the WTO General Assembly will go ahead as planned in Beijing in three months time - in the course of which the World Tourism Organization would be transformed into a specialized agency of the United Nations.

This historical world tourism summit will send a signal of confidence and support from WTO to the nation of China, to the Asian tourism industry, and to all our members in the region. We in WTO are convinced that the Asia-Pacific tourism industry is coming back on track and will soon re-emerge as it once was — a vigorous and powerful engine for economic development in the entire region.

Thank you.

# 20

# PATA—Acceptance Speech

1. As I stand here today to thank you for the honour bestowed on me, I am overwhelmed by the significance of the occasion.

2. This is the 50th Year of PATA. This also marks the beginning of PATA's entry into the 21st Century. Naturally today, we tend to look back to the years that have gone by and also look at the future - always in expectations and sometimes in apprehension, but always in hope.

3. As I look back, I marvel at the wisdom and vision of the few individuals who joined in 1952 to start this remarkable journey which as **James Michener** has said "accomplished more than any other travel organisation in educating and marketing Pacific travel....... environmentally, socially and culturally". When half the world was talking only about the commanding heights of the public sector as a guiding economic philosophy, they were clearly visionaries ahead of their .time who could think of a systematic private-public partnership at that time. But, the changes in the geo-political situations in the last 50 years have changed tourism scenario beyond our wildest dreams. The cold war is behind us. New political alignments and unions like the European Union and NAFTA have emerged. The Soviet Union and Eastern Europe have changed. The Korean wars and the Vietnam War have gone to the shadows of the past. But, above all, as you all know, changes in civil aviation technologies in the later part of the last century revolutionised travel and tourism to an extent

that it has emerged as the biggest industry of the world. Most of you have been part of that history and many of you have helped in shaping the future. But, in the general euphoria about the future, we must keep our heads clear about the pitfalls on the way, as the jolts of East Asian crisis made us aware. I believe PATA must continue to act as the collective forum for introspection and for continuous evaluation and revaluation.

4. While the wisdom, experience and tenacity of all of you have put PATA in the position that it is today, we need to draw on all that experience to face the future challenges. The technological revolutions particularly in information technology have made the world a truly global village and will change travel and tourism for ever. Concept of time and space have collapsed, cultural boundaries have evaporated. Travel and tourism sector, it is predicted, will see the globalisation process accompanied by increased concentration and vertical integration of the private sector. Tourism business is becoming more global. Mergers, acquisitions and integrations are changing business relationships. Technological factors have been mentioned as one of the factors affecting even PATA-PATA members relationship, we were told, were affected by technological factors. What role will PATA play in harnessing the power of the emerging and fast changing technologies to strengthen the primary role that it has played in marketing? PATA will, no doubt, have to think deeply about this primary challenge of the 21st Century - of being in tune with the spirit of change and providing leadership to all the members for a cohesive move to benefit from the technological development.

5. But, it is the human mind that guides Technology I realise that marketing has been critical to PATA's evolution and in fact its forte. Even the dimension and content of marketing is fast changing. At the core of all our activities are the people. Tourism is about people. People's attitude, habits are changing, as they certainly would in this new era of

technology. As we go forward, we would like to be guided by your needs, by your perception about the future and by your ideas about what the people want and what PATA should do put this concern at the core of its future strategy. PATA has always been moulded by its members visions. I would like to see a truly interactive system evolving where your new ideas, and innovative strategies get reflection. After all, it is the human mind that is behind all those technological revolutions.

6. In this context, we have to think about how to expand our family and strengthen our resource base. The PATA - PATA Chapter relationship has to be set on a solid foundation, on shared ideology and commitment, on shouldering together of the responsibilities. A vibrant dynamic relationship of this wider family based on the pride of belonging and the privilege of sharing should be our launching pad for the 21st Century initiatives.

7. I had talked about people and the need to divert our concern to people rather than numbers. I am delighted to find that this humane concern has been the motivating philosophy of PATA from the very beginning. In the very first conference, **Earl Warren** had spoken that the objective of all this growth was peace - "first, last and always". From 1952 to 1992, the vision of travel as a noble and humanising activity run through all PATA activities. In this same place, Hong Kong, in 1992 Ken Chamberlain had talked about qualitative long-term approach to tourism and PATA's continuing role in trying to make this world a better place to be. At no time, this philosophy needed more reiteration than today. We need to focus on the positive impact of tourism as a desirable catalyst for development. We have, from different parts of the world many good examples of tourism and travel creating public awareness for sustainable development. We need to spread this message to wider areas. We need to evolve a code of ethics that will be our distinguishing badge of leadership in Travel and Tourism.

8. Sometimes back while looking at the future, "Direction 2000 for PATA" talked about going beyond the region and of evolving a philosophy that is global in its sweep. As technology has made a global village of this world, I feel that such a desire is only but natural. Of course, dovetailing global outlook with regional orientation will raise many issues for debate and discussions. All living and dynamic organizations grow with such internal debates. I personally always liked to say "Ah, but a man's reach should exceed his grasp or what is heaven for?" I know, there are many other regional, international organizations who are our fellow travellers and who share our ideologies. We will stand to gain by forging honourable relationship with them. I shall be delighted to have your guidance on these thoughts, as we go along.

9. I seek your indulgence to make a personal reference at this stage. I was pleasantly surprised to find that about a decade back in Hong Kong you had honoured my distinguished friend Shri Inder Sharma as Chairman of PATA. This coincidence apart I accept this honour bestowed on me also as an honour for my country. India, as you know, is a country, which as Albert Einstien said, "taught us how to count, without which no worthwhile scientific discovery could have been made."

10. Mark Twain thought, "India is the most extraordinary country that the Sun visits on his round." The French scholar, Romain Rolland thought this "is a place where all the dreams of living men have found a home from the very earliest days when man began the dream of existence". The German philosopher Max Mueller had echoed almost the same feeling. "And when you return from India in 2002, you will agree, as did Madam Chu, that it indeed is an enriching experience.

11. I have intentionally not mentioned the various on-going projects and programmes of PATA because our very able team headed* by the CEO Joe Mclnerney have already extensively briefed you.

12. I must thank you all once again for honouring me with the mantle of Chairmanship at an exciting time in PATA's history. I humbly accept the task and seek your assistance in sincerely carrying forward the glorious tradition our organisation. Terry Francis had referred in Manila to the "Can do" spirit of PATA. I would only like to endorse the same with the words of poet Virgil -

"They can
Because
They think
They can."

I think we can.

Thank you.

And I am pleased to announce my officers for this year. They are Chairman-Elect Mr. John Sanford, Secretary - Treasure Mr. Bo. W. Long.

# 21

# PATA: Handing Over Speech

His Excellency, the Prime Minister of Malaysia, respected Ministers, excellencies,

Ladies and Gentlemen.

I know, having to speak after such a scintillating show and after such an inspiring speech of His Excellency, the Prime Minister, anything I say may sound pedestrian. Still, if I gather the courage to run that risk, it is only to thank you sincerely, respected Prime Minister, for being with us on this happy and historic occasion and for providing dignity and pride to our belonging with your gracious presence.

It is only fitting that we should be celebrating the 50th Anniversary of PATA and be talking about our proud past and the promising future here in Kuala Lumpur, because this is one place where under your leadership the Asian economic dream started taking shape. It is also amazing that 50 years back a group of visionaries could see what the world is recognizing today at the turn of the century, that Asia Pacific is destined to lead the global economy into the next century. In the first conference when Earl Warren had told the delegates that "much of the world's history is to be written in the Pacific area" he was almost prophetic.

Out of that vision was born this Organization which, as rightly stated by novelist James Michener, accomplished more than any other organization in educating and marketing Pacific travel environmentally, socially and culturally. PATA is proud of its expertise in absorbing the market potential for the greater good of the greatest number in Asia Pacific which borders 75% of the world's population. PATA is equally proud that we pursue this development goal with a conscience. Right from day one, concern for a qualitative long-term approach to tourism and a desire to use the resources and expertise to make this, world a better place to be, has dominated all activities of PATA.

Asia with its spending' power, its dominance in new technology and expanding capital resources, has all the potentials for propelling growth in the region.

At the time of independence of India, the country I come from, one of the five dreams of the great philosopher Aurobindo was "for the resurgence and liberation of the peoples of Asia and her return to a great role in the progress of human civilization". You are at the forefront of the Asian economic resurgence trying to mould our pride to shape a better future.

Way back in 1915 the Russian artist Malevich 'presented the unpresentable' by painting a white square on a white background. Malevich said "I have beaten the lining of the coloured sky, torn it away and in the sack which formed itself, I have put colours and knotted it. Swim! The free white sea, infinity, lies before you."*

Things have changed since. Shrinking time and space, disappearing barriers of borders have given shape to that soaring, roving, liberal human spirit. People are traveling more, the number more than doubling since 1980. The future is expected to see still greater exponential growth making travel and tourism not only the biggest industry in the global village that the world has become but also the most potent tool for development and peace. This was the dream of the founding fathers of PATA — reflecting the saying of Mahatma Gandhi — that "travel is the language of peace".

But we have challenges to face. We have to ensure that this global village cares for people more than profit.

---

* Chakraverty, Sauvik : Antidote. Essays against Indian Socialism.

Technologies changing at an ever accelerating pace may put those countries at a disadvantage which do not have the capacity or the resources to adopt so quickly to the changes. We have already seen lengthening shadows of increasing inequality co-existing with growing prosperity of the world. During the period that tourism has almost doubled, sixty countries of the world have been getting poorer. The income gap between the fifth of the world living in the richest countries and the fifth in the poorest has been increasing. We have the daunting challenge of adjusting our development needs to environmental compulsions, of putting ethics and human rights at the core of our concern. With its ever present 'can-do' spirit PATA, as always will be at the forefront to meet these emerging challenges. We feel encouraged, your excellency, by your presence and patronage, for that journey of ours.

On behalf of the entire PATA community, I would like to thank you the respected Prime Minister, your government and the people of Malaysia for such warm hospitality and welcome.

We had a fantastic evening of colour and culture yesterday. We have heard many stories of Malaysia's achievements, but we could not believe that you could even command a special appearance by the full moon.

We are happy Malaysia tourism is doing so well. Personally, I understand, the Indians have contributed generously to this growth. Because India and Malaysia have always been together in the old and as well as the new Asian dreams, I hope by the time PATA meets next year in New Delhi, Malaysia would be a major contributor to our growth. With sound economic reforms, rebust economic growth and financial stability, India is well on .the way to fulfill its economic potential and expectations. The PATA road from Kuala Lumpur to New Delhi may be that partnership for Asia Pacific to write the history of the world as Earl Warren had predicted in the first conference.